Richard B. Cook

The early and later Delaware Baptists

Richard B. Cook

The early and later Delaware Baptists

ISBN/EAN: 9783743327115

Manufactured in Europe, USA, Canada, Australia, Japa

Cover: Foto ©ninafisch / pixelio.de

Manufactured and distributed by brebook publishing software (www.brebook.com)

Richard B. Cook

The early and later Delaware Baptists

THE

EARLY AND LATER

DELAWARE BAPTISTS.

BY

REV. RICHARD B. COOK, A. M.,

PASTOR OF THE SECOND BAPTIST CHURCH, WILMINGTON,
DELAWARE.

PHILADELPHIA:
AMERICAN BAPTIST PUBLICATION SOCIETY,
1420 CHESTNUT STREET.

PREFACE.

At the meeting of the Delaware Baptist Union, at Media, Pennsylvania, November, 1879, an outline of "The Early and Later Delaware Baptists" was read, whereupon a Committee, consisting of Prof. G. D. B. Pepper, D. D., Rev. George Bradford, and Rev. William H. Young, was appointed by the "Union" to confer with the author and secure its publication in full.

The author gratefully acknowledges his indebtedness for books of reference, pamphlets, and manuscripts to the Hon. H. G. Jones, P. Miles Frame, Esq., Elder E. Rittenhouse, Rev. B. MacMackin; and for the most of the facts relating to the organizations, pastors, etc. of the early Baptist churches in Delaware, such as Welsh Tract, Duck Creek, Gravelly Branch, Mispillion, etc., he is indebted to the manuscript materials of Rev. Morgan Edwards, which are preserved in the Library of the American Baptist Historical Society, Philadelphia.

The author returns his acknowledgments to Louis H. Everts, publisher of *The Baptist Encyclopædia*—which he is now issuing under the editorial care of Wm. Cathcart, D. D.—for electrotypes of Abel Morgan, D. D., Daniel Dodge, D. D., and Rev. R .B. Cook; also to J. C. Harkness, A. M., of Harkness Academy, Wilmington, for the electrotype of Welsh Baptist Church.

INTRODUCTION.

By Prof. G. D. B. PEPPER, D. D.,
Crozer Theological Seminary, Delaware Co., Penn.

INSPIRATION teaches us to forget the things which are behind, to reach forth unto those things which are before, and to press toward the mark. And well may it; for to us, in the future only is achievement possible. The past will not come to us, nor shall we go to it. But to run well we must run not blindly, but intelligently. And as we know the future only by a study of the past, we must look back, in order to see ahead. Practical Wisdom ever lights her torch at the flame of history; thus he who best remembers "things which are behind" for instruction, best forgets them for attainment. This is clearly seen from the structure of Holy Scripture, in which historical record is dominant in influence and predominant in quantity. From out that book homely and lowly events, told in a plain and simple way, cast a guiding light for all the ages to come.

This little *History of the Delaware Baptists* thus commends itself in the very fact that it is a *history*. And truly it well deserves the name. The author, admirably qualified and situated for its preparation, has spared no time, labor, or expense to make it an exact exhibit of the actual course of events. His facts are not his inventions. Hence the lesson brought to us is not his, but theirs. Hence the voice which speaks to us is that, not of man, but of providence, which is the voice of God.

Yet the book is not a mere heap of dead facts, a pile of dry bones. History is a life. Historic events are the result and manifestation of spirit and power. They are bound together organically by a vital principle, and constitute a genuine development. Were this not so, they would have no meaning for living men in the guidance of their lives. The writer of history recognizes this life, grasps, holds, and shows it, and thus aids his readers in understanding the past. So does this little work come to us, not simply as a depository of facts, but also as a manifestation of their principle and meaning.

The presentation, though concise, is clear, impartial, and comprehensive.

Baptist history in Delaware has a character and value all its own. It is unique. It is not distinguished simply by the place of its enactment, a corner cut off from a uniform piece of cloth. Its lessons are its own, and it teaches them in its own way. One lesson, especially, of utmost import it makes solemnly and sadly prominent. Perhaps nowhere else in this country has Antinomianism, with its natural, if not inseparable, attendants of anti-Missionism, anti-Sunday-school-ism, and all the other kindred *anti-isms*, so impressively by its fruits proved its origin, nature, and doom. In doing this it has also proved with like certainty its antagonism to the genuine Baptist faith and practice. While the earliest and the latest Baptists are one in spirit and doctrine, they are both irreconcilably in antagonism with this distortion of divine truth. Its defenders may claim and receive the Baptist name, but they have no right to it. It does not belong to them. That they wear it works mischief to those to whom it does belong, for it leads many to confound the true with the false, and unjustly to regard the true as they justly do the false.

But while this defection carries its lesson of humiliation and warning, there remains much equally instructive of which to be proud. Heroic men, able ministers of the New Testament, with fellow-workers of kindred spirit all astir with Christian enterprise, their hearts and hands always ready for every good work, sowed good seed in the soil of Delaware. That enemies from their own number, bearing their own name, afterward sowed tares almost to the destruction of the wheat, was not their fault. The record of their lives and works is an ample vindication of the Baptist name, and will be an inspiration to Baptist workers.

Delaware needs, what God is giving her, a revival of the old cause and a resurrection of its old champions. Dr. J. D. Fulton once said that "a Baptist Church is an illuminated edition of the New Testament." Of the true idea of a Baptist Church, fully realized, this is hardly too much to say. Its members are all members of Christ's spiritual body. Its Head is Christ, and him only. Its law is the New Testament itself. Its authoritative Interpreter of the law is the Holy Spirit, so enlightening all as to secure harmony of view and action. Its officers are presbyters, or bishops, and deacons. Its ordinances are the two prescribed in the New Testament, observed as there given, administered to those only for whom they were given, to express the great spiritual facts and truths committed to them, and observed in the order fixed alike by their own nature and the word of inspiration. It holds itself and each of its members bound to do everything possible to put the gospel into all human hearts and forms of human life all the world over. Catholic in sympathies, its members love all God's children, whatever their names, and are ready to co-operate with them or anybody else in all good works, but refuse to countenance a subversion of Christ's revealed will, whether intentional or unintentional. This ideal church may be rare, but the present Baptists of Delaware intend to make it easy to find just such a church anywhere in the State. This little volume is intended and is well fitted to become a help to this end.

CONTENTS.

	PAGE
I. THE EARLY BAPTIST CHURCHES.......	14
1. The Welsh Tract Church, 1701.....................	14
2. Labors of Baker and Hughes, 1775...............	22
3. The Sounds Church, 1779...........................	27
4. Broad Creek Church, 1781..........................	28
5. Cow Marsh Church, 1781............................	30
6. Bryn Zion Church, 1781.............................	31
7. Mispillion Church, 1783–1848....................	34
8. Gravelly Branch Church, 1785....................	37
9. The Bethel...	38
10. First Church, Wilmington, 1785...................	40
11. Distinguished Men...................................	51
12. The Delaware Association, 1795..................	74
II. THE LATER BAPTIST CHURCHES........	96
1. Second Church, Wilmington, 1835...............	96
2. Dover Church, 1852.................................	103
3. First German Church, Wilmington, 1856......	107
4. Delaware Avenue Church, Wilmington, 1865.	112

CONTENTS.

PAGE

5. Plymouth Church, 1867–1873...................... 115
6. Lincoln Church, 1869–1873....................... 117
7. Zion Church, 1871................................ 118
8. Wyoming Church, 1872............................ 120
9. Magnolia Church, 1873........................... 121
10. Milford Church, 1873............................ 122
11. Elm Street Church, Wilmington, 1873–1876... 123
12. Shiloh Church, Wilmington, 1876................ 123
13. New Castle Church, 1876......................... 124
14. Bethany Church, 1878............................ 127
15. Wilmington Baptist City Mission, 1870......... 130
16. Wyoming Institute, 1869......................... 130
17. Delaware Baptist Union, 1878.................... 132

III. CONCLUSION 143

THE EARLY AND LATER DELAWARE BAPTISTS.

In the fall of 1682, William Penn sailed up the Delaware to take charge in person of his large estates in the New World. He landed first at New Castle, Delaware, and then went on to Philadelphia. There were Baptists among the early settlers of Pennsylvania, for the Cold Spring Baptist Church was formed in 1685, and in 1688 the oldest existing Baptist Church in Pennsylvania, the Lower Dublin, at Pennypack, now in Philadelphia. The "Old Swedes' Church," Wilmington, regarded as "among the antiquities of American civilization," was built in 1698, or ten years later. As early as 1703 a Baptist Church existed in Delaware. The Baptist churches first formed in this State were mostly of Welsh origin. The earlier churches became eventually Antinomian in doctrine and practice, but the later churches have always been missionary. For other reasons, therefore, besides those of convenience and of origin, we treat them separately. At one period of their history these early churches were one in doctrine and practice with the Baptist churches of to-day.

I.—THE EARLY BAPTIST CHURCHES.

1. The Welsh Tract Church, 1701.

For the origin of this, the first Baptist Church in the State, we must cross the Atlantic to Wales. In the spring of 1701, sixteen Baptists in the counties of Pembroke and Caermarthen resolved to go to America. They formed themselves into a church, with Rev. Thomas Griffith, one of their number, as Pastor. They embarked at Milford Haven in June, 1701, and have been properly styled a "church emigrant." They landed at Philadelphia, September 8, 1701, where they were courteously received by the brethren, and advised to settle about Pennypack, to which place they removed. They continued at Pennypack about a year and a half, during which time their church increased

WELSH TRACT BAPTIST CHURCH,
From Hill near Newark.   P. 14.

from sixteen to thirty-seven. Then they "took up" land in New Castle County—one of the three counties of Delaware then in Pennsylvania—from Messrs. Evans, Davis, and Willis, who had purchased upward of thirty thousand acres of William Penn, called the "Welsh Tract." To this they removed in 1703, leaving some of their number at Pennypack, and receiving while there accessions in return. At Iron Hill they built a small meeting-house, which occupied the site upon which the present one, erected in 1746, stands. It is in the neighborhood of Newark. In the yard around the church sleep the successive generations that have in their time and turn worshipped in that place. The new church was joined from time to time by others from Pennypack and from Wales. Many also united with them by baptism; and, being aggressive, their principles soon spread in Delaware, and also into the adjacent parts of Pennsylvania and Maryland, and as far as South Carolina. The Welsh Tract Church was the mother of the London Tract (Pennsylvania) and the Duck Creek (Delaware) churches, and in some degree of the Wilmington, Cow Marsh, and Mispillion churches (Delaware), since her pastors labored successfully in these latter places, and many of the converts, having united with that church, were dismissed at times to form the churches that were organized in these fields.

In November, 1736, forty-eight members, says Edwards, under the leadership of Rev. Abel Morgan, "late of Middletown," were dismissed to form the Welsh Neck Church, on Pedee River, South Carolina, where they had settled. Benedict gives James James, whose son Philip became their Pastor, as their leader, and as the date of the settlement 1737, and that of the formation of the church January, 1738, and says that the number was thirty when organized. When he wrote, it was the largest as well as the oldest church in the Welsh Neck Association, which was composed of thirty-eight churches, and was the mother of all the churches in that region.*

But to return. Says Morgan Edwards, in his manuscript ("Materials toward a History of the Baptists of Delaware," pp. 232, 233): "Welsh Tract Church was the principal, if not sole, means of introducing singing, imposition

* Benedict's *History of the Baptists*, pp. 704, 705, 710.

of hands, church covenants, etc. among the Baptists in the Middle States. The *Century* Confession was in America before the year 1716, but without the articles which relate to those subjects." "That year they were inserted by Rev. Abel Morgan, who translated the Confession into Welsh, after being signed by one hundred and twenty-two of the members of the Welsh Tract Church. They were inserted in the next English edition, and adopted with the other articles by the Association [Philadelphia] of 1742. Singing psalms met with opposition, especially at Cohansey, but laying on of hands on baptized believers, as such, gained acceptance with more difficulty, as appears from the following history, translated from 'Welsh Tract Church Book'— that is, the church record, which up to 1732 was kept in Welsh: 'We could not be in fellowship (at the Lord's Table) with our brethren in Pennepek and Philadelphia, because they did not hold to the *laying-on-of-hands* (on baptized believers) and some other particulars (as to church covenants, ruling elders, etc.) relating to a church.'"

The difficulty increased, owing to the presence among them of members who had joined them at Pennypack. It was settled by deputies at the house of Richard Miles, Radnor, Pennsylvania, June 22, 1706, on the side of mutual forbearance, liberty, and union. When an effort was made three years after by some to reopen the matter, the church refused, saying, "We are satisfied that all was right, by the good effects that followed, for from that time forward our brethren held sweet communion together at the Lord's Table, and our minister was invited to preach and assisted at an ordination at Pennepek after the death of our brother Watts. He proceeded from thence to the Jerseys, where he enlightened many in the good ways of the Lord, insomuch that, in three years after, all the ministers and about fifty-five private members had submitted to the ordinance." So it appears from Edwards, in the extract above, that the Welsh Tract Church numbered at least one hundred and twenty-two in 1716.

Benedict says (page 304): "The church is very handsomely endowed." According to Edwards, the endowment yielded an annual income of one hundred pounds, or about five hundred dollars. The pulpit was filled by good and able men of Welsh extraction for about seventy years. The following is a list of the Pastors of the church, with dates indicating the period of their service, and in the order of their succession, as far as we can ascertain: Rev. Thomas Griffith * was born in Wales in 1645, and emigrated with the church, which he served as Pastor for twenty-four years. He died at Pennypack July 25, 1725. He visited New Jersey in 1706 and 1711, and taught the people, stirring up young men to use their gifts, and thus many churches were soon supplied with pastors from their own members.

Rev. Elisha Thomas was born in Wales in 1674, and emigrated with the church, being one of its constituent members. He died Nov. 7, 1730, and was buried in the churchyard, "where," says Edwards, "a handsome tomb is erected to his memory." This tomb, still preserved, would hardly be regarded now, after the lapse of one hundred and fifty years, as being "handsome" with its rude carvings of an open Bible and inscriptions—

"With uncouth rhymes and shapeless sculpture decked."

* Mr. Edwards writes this name Griffiths.

Rev. Enoch Morgan, the next Pastor, was also a constituent member of the church, and came over with them. He was a half-brother to Rev. Benjamin Griffith, Pastor of Montgomery Baptist Church, Pennsylvania, who was also for years Moderator of the Philadelphia Association, and a brother of the Rev. Abel Morgan, author of the Welsh Concordance. Their father was a famous Baptist minister in Wales, named Morgan ap Rhyddarch. Enoch Morgan was born in Wales in 1676, died March 25, 1740, and was buried in the churchyard at Welsh Tract, where his tomb still stands.

Rev. Owen Thomas was born in Wales in 1676, and came to America in 1707. He became Pastor in 1740, resigned in 1748, and died in 1760. He was "held in dear remembrance by all that knew him," and was styled "an excellent man."

Rev. David Davis, born in Wales in 1708, came to America in 1710, was baptized January, 1729, and ordained at Welsh Tract, 1734, at which time he became Pastor, serving the church thirty-five years. He died in 1769, and was buried in the graveyard of the church, where "a handsome stone covers his remains also."

Rev. John Sutton was the first Pastor of the church who was born in America. He became Pastor, November 3, 1770, and resigned to go to Virginia in 1777. He was a native of New Jersey, and a man of considerable distinction.

Rev. John Boggs, his successor, was an able-bodied man, says the Chronicle, hence he travelled much, preaching in the surrounding country. He was born in 1741, bred a Presbyterian, baptized at Welsh Tract, November 3, 1771, was ordained and took charge of the church, December 5, 1781, and died there in 1802.

Rev. Gideon Farrell was born in Talbot County, Maryland, in 1763. He was bred a Quaker, but was baptized by Philip Hughes in 1770 at the Sounds, and ordained at Churchill in 1779. Mr. Farrell had preached about once a month for the church for seven years, aiding the Pastor, before he was invested with the pastoral office. He remained Pastor until his death, in 1820 or 1821.

Rev. Stephen W. Woolford served them from 1822 to 1830.*

---

* Taken from the Minutes of the Delaware Association. The Delaware Association Minutes for 1837, '38, '73, and '76 inaccessible.

Elder Samuel Trott, from 1831 to 1832.*—Elder William K. Robinson from 1833 to 1836,* or later. He died in 1843 or 1844.—Elder Thomas Barton from 1839* until his death in 1869 or 1870. He had then been sixty years in the Christian ministry, forty-five of which were spent within the bounds of the Delaware Association as Pastor of three of its churches.—Elder G. W. Staton in 1871 and 1872.*—Elder William Grafton appears as Pastor in 1877.—No Pastor in 1879.†

2. LABORS OF BAKER AND HUGHES, 1778.

There came from Virginia into Delaware, at the close of 1778, Rev. Elijah Baker, and in the spring of 1779 he was followed by Rev. Philip Hughes from the same State. They labored together "as evangelists" for about twelve months, preaching at Broad Creek, Gravelly Branch, and other places. Many

---

* Taken from the Minutes of the Delaware Association. The Delaware Association Minutes for 1837, '38, '73, and '76 inaccessible.

† As far as can be learned from the Minutes of the Delaware Association accessible to the writer, this is a correct list. If there is any error, doubtless it occurs after 1870, to which date it is accurate.

converts were "baptized on profession of faith and repentance." They prepared materials and resolved to build churches. At first they and their disciples went by the name of Separate Baptists, but the distinction was soon dropped. They were not only well received and their labors approved, but, in their efforts to save souls, were aided on every hand by Baptist ministers and laymen, who helped them also in the constitution of churches and in the ordination of ministers. And none were more zealous in this united effort than Messrs. John Boggs and Thomas Fleeson, Pastors respectively of Welsh Tract and London Tract churches.

Messrs. Baker and Hughes were instrumental in founding twenty-one churches in Virginia, Maryland, and Delaware, and spent much time in "visiting them, as fathers do their children." The Salisbury Association was organized by them. It takes its name from a town in Maryland near the Delaware line, where this Association was formed, and distinguished as the birthplace of Rev. Noah Davis, the founder of the American Baptist Publication Society.

Mr. Baker's life is recorded both by J. B. Taylor, D. D., in his *Lives of Virginia Baptist*

Ministers, and Rev. R. B. Semple in his *History of the Rise and Progress of the Baptists in Virginia*. The latter publishes a letter from Dr. Robert Lemon, for years Moderator of the Salisbury Association, at whose house he died November 6, 1798, testifying to his exalted Christian character, the faithfulness and power of his preaching, and his triumph in the hour of death, when he "seemed rather to be translated than to suffer pain in his dissolution"—(p. 397). Morgan Edwards, in his "Materials . . . Delaware," pp. 247, 248, gives us an interesting account as to how Mr. Baker came to leave Virginia, where he was born in 1742, and baptized by the famous Samuel Harris in 1769, and where he suffered much for the word of God. He came into Delaware upon "an invitation from Thomas Batston, Esq., who had heard him preach through the grates in Accomac jail about the year 1777. The rude Virginians, in order to get rid of him, put him on board a privateer, where he suffered much abuse, but he continued to sing, and pray, and exhort notwithstanding, till the crew was tired, and then let him alone, saying, 'He is not worth a curse;' but the privateer being detained long in the harbor by contrary wind, the crew suspected that the cause was that preaching fellow, and therefore put him on board another vessel; but the wind continuing contrary, that vessel began to be of the same mind with the privateer, and therefore shifted him to a third, and the third put him ashore. When Jonah found himself on the dry land he complied with Squire Batston's invitation." And be it said to the credit of Delaware that she had no prison, like Virginia, nor whipping-post, like Massachusetts, for Baptists, who were left undisturbed in their views and practices. And Delaware has to thank for this liberty her governor, William Penn, whose father, Admiral Penn of the English navy, tradition says, was a Baptist. And Penn was only exemplifying the time-honored Baptist principle of equal liberty for all when he came to establish "a civil society of men enjoying the highest degree of freedom and happiness."

The account that Mr. Edwards gives of Mr. Baker's co-laborer is not without interest. He says: "Rev. Philip Hughes shares in the praise of Mr. Baker, as they were fellow-laborers in most of the good that was done in this and other States. He was born in Colver County, November 28, 1750, bred a Churchman, avowed his present sentiments, August 10, 1773, when he was baptized by Rev. David Thompson, called to the ministry in Rowanty Church, was ordained at an Association held in Virginia, August 13, 1776. . . . He published a volume of hymns in 1782, many of which are of his own composing; also an answer to a Virginia clergyman on the subject of baptism in 1784. He also was obliged twice to appear on the stage to dispute on the subject—once at Fouling Creek in Maryland in 1782. His antagonist was a Methodist preacher of the name of Willis. Victory was announced by both parties, but facts varied much, for after the dispute three class-leaders and many others were baptized by Mr. Hughes. The other dispute was held near the mouth of [the] Potomac, in Virginia, in the year 1785. Mr. Hughes's challenger was one Coles, another Methodist preacher. Here the victory was decisive, for twenty-two of the audience were baptized the next day, and soon after as many more by Rev. Lewis Lunsford."—*Materials, Del.*, pp. 248, 249.

3. The Sounds Church, 1779.

The second Baptist Church in Delaware was the Sounds, in Baltimore Hundred, Sussex County. In 1791 it had no "temporalities," no meeting-house, no fixed salary. They held their meetings in the dwellings of Tull and Wilegoos. It has ceased to exist. It was formed August 12, 1779, with twenty-five members, through the labors of Messrs. Baker and Hughes, and was one of the ten that formed the Salisbury Association in 1782. From this church, says Edwards, sprang six ministers: John, Samuel, and Jonathan Gibbins, Eliphaz Dazey, Gideon Farrell, and Edward Carter Dingle, the latter a son of a clergyman of the Church of England. Messrs. Baker and Hughes first supplied it with preaching; then the neighboring pastors. The Rev. Jonathan Gibbins was their first Pastor. He was born in Broad Creek Hundred, December 16, 1751; called to the ministry in this church, and ordained April 16, 1787, by Rev. Messrs. Hughes and Dazey, when he assumed pastoral charge of this and of the Broad Creek Church.

4. Broad Creek Church, 1781.

This church was in Sussex County, and was the third organized in the State. It was constituted May 31, 1781, through the labors of Messrs. Hughes and Baker, with forty-seven members. In 1791 they had no house of worship, but worshipped in the dwellings of the members in rotation, and had the Lord's Supper administered quarterly. The minister's "income, twenty pounds, including perquisites." It helped to form the Salisbury Association. It decreased in ten years from forty-seven to twenty-three, because several families emigrated hence to Georgia and other Southern parts about the year 1784, and a considerable number were detached to form a church, in 1785, at Gravelly Branch. The first ministers of this church were its founders. Rev. John Gibbins was the first Pastor. He was born in the neighborhood, raised a Presbyterian, and was one of the first converts of Messrs. Baker and Hughes. He was called to the ministry by the Sounds Church. After his ordination at Fouling Creek he travelled abroad till 1784, when he returned and became Pastor of this church. He remedied the defects of his early education by personal industry so far as to be master of his mother tongue. Says Morgan Edwards ("Materials, Delaware," p. 253): "In a conversation I had with him in 1786 he lamented that he could not read his Testament in the language of Christ and his apostles, rather than depend on translations, without which knowledge of Greek he deemed it impossible to study the gospel critically. He was therefore determined to visit Rhode Island College, but the small-pox broke his resolution at Wilmington, where he died in 1786." This shows that special training for the gospel ministry was appreciated in Delaware at an early day. He was brother to Rev. Samuel Gibbins, to whose labors the churches in Sussex County, Delaware, and in other States, owe great obligation. Of the Gibbins family, as of the household of Stephanas, it may be said, "They have addicted themselves to the ministry of the saints."

His successor, Rev. John Benson, was born in Worcester County, Maryland. He was bred a Presbyterian. After he became a Baptist he employed himself in reading sermons to the people when no minister happened to be present, and afterward began to preach in the assemblies of the church. He continued this course till June 14, 1790, when he was ordained by Rev. Messrs. Hughes, John Pollard, Jonathan Gibbins, and Edward Carter Dingle, and at once took pastoral charge of this church in conjunction with that of Gravelly Branch. He was assisted in his work by Deacon Joshua Gibbins. He died in 1818 or '19.

Rev. Joseph Flood, born at Welsh Tract, November 2, 1767, converted and baptized there in 1790, and ordained at Cow Marsh, December 11, 1791, became Pastor, August 11, 1792.

5. Cow Marsh Church, 1781.

The fourth church constituted was the Cow Marsh (or Mount Moriah) Church, in Kent County, July 18, 1781. John Sutton, Pastor at Welsh Tract, preached here in 1780. Then Messrs. Isaac Stelle, R. Kelsay, William Worth, and others performed a like service. In 1782, James Sutton came and baptized. Others were baptized here and at Welsh Tract, and twenty-six were formed into a church by Messrs. Boggs and Fleeson. Seven of these were from the

Welsh Tract Church. They joined the Philadelphia Association in 1786; had no house of worship in 1791, but met for worship at the dwelling of Job Meredith, Sr. They were preparing to build in 1781, and had a considerable sum subscribed, but their active friend, Luff Meredith, died, when the design was abandoned. They were talking of putting it into execution when Edwards wrote in 1791. The Mispillion is in part the offspring of this church. Rev. Eliphaz Dazey became Pastor, April 21, 1787, taking upon him also the oversight of the Duck Creek Church. He was born October 26, 1754, in Sussex County, Delaware, and ordained July 12, 1784. He resigned October 25, 1788, but revisited them for a considerable time. Messrs. Farrell and Dewees administered the ordinances among them for some time.

6. Bryn Zion Church, 1781.

The Duck Creek (or Bryn Zion) Church, Kent County, was organized November 24, 1781. It was a branch of the Welsh Tract Church from 1733 until its constitution into a church. This church consisted of three branches—the one near Duck Creek, another at East Landing, and the third at Georgetown. The latter branch originated through the preaching of Messrs. Fleeson and Boggs, who went there by invitation of a Mr. Parsons, a Methodist. They repeated their visit, and other ministers succeeded them, until sixteen persons were converted and baptized, and joined the Duck Creek Church.

The tract of land known as Duck Creek Hundred was settled in 1733 by a number of Welsh families, some of them Independents and some Baptists. Of the Baptists, there were eight or ten families who came from the Welsh Tract. The Independents had a church and a house, which they called Mount Zion. This church wasted away, and the Baptists worshipped in their house while it stood, and rebuilt it in 1771, when the lot was conveyed to them. The house was of brick, thirty by twenty-five feet, and, as the historian says, "accommodated with a stove." It still stands, and is in the neighborhood of Smyrna. They had preaching before their organization by Rev. Enoch Morgan, Rev. Hugh Davis of the Great Valley, Pennsylvania, and Rev. David Davis of Welsh Tract. Rev. Griffith Jones settled among them in 1749, and continued until his death in 1754. In the spring of 1766 Rev. William Davis of New Britain, Pennsylvania, settled among them, but soon died. Then Rev. Messrs. David Davis, John Sutton, John Boggs, and others ministered there till they numbered thirty in all, when they petitioned the Welsh Tract Church for permission to become a separate church, having continued a branch of the Welsh Tract for forty-eight years —1733 to 1781—and were received into the Philadelphia Association in 1786. In 1791 the membership was seventy-four, and the minister's revenue was eighty pounds, or about four hundred dollars. While the Independent Church flourished the Baptists often worshipped and had administered to them the Lord's Supper in private houses, as in those of James Hyatt and Evan David Hughs. Their Pastors after organization were Rev. Eliphaz Dazey, who resigned October 25, 1787, and Rev. Messrs. James Jones, John Patten, and Gideon Farrell, who were co-Pastors. Dr. and Rev. James Jones was born at Welsh Tract, April 6, 1756, and died in 1829. He was there licensed to preach November 2, 1782, and was educated at Newark Academy, where he also, as Edwards says, studied "physic." April 7, 1789, he took joint oversight of the church with Rev. John Patten, who was ordained the same day. The latter was born at Cow Marsh, December 15, 1752, and called to the ministry and licensed by the church there June 14, 1788. Rev. Gideon Farrell, associated with them, has been mentioned in connection with the Welsh Tract Church.

7. MISPILLION CHURCH, 1783–1848.

The Mispillion, in Kent County, was the sixth church, and was organized May 10, 1783. Messrs. Boggs and Fleeson preached there in 1781. They repeated their visits, and baptized some candidates, five of whom joined the church at Cow Marsh. Messrs. Baker and Hughes then labored here and baptized, when twenty converts were collected and constituted a church. They joined the Philadelphia Association in 1785, but in 1789 requested release to unite with the Salisbury Association. They had no house in 1791, and worshipped in the house of C. Dewees. Says Mr. Edwards (p. 270): "This church hath, in eight years, decreased from twenty to eleven, owing to deaths, emigrations, and no additions equal to losses; and it is to be feared it will soon cease to be, as their minister intends going to the Western World;" by which was probably meant Ohio. The church continued to exist, however, and it was not until 1848 that its name disappeared from the Minutes of the Delaware Association. The Rev. A. S. Bastian, Milford, near which the Mispillion Church is located, sends the following particulars: The church was incorporated in 1796, when they began to build their first meeting-house. They met for business on Saturday noon, when they usually had a sermon. The first board of Trustees consisted of Peter King, Vincent Beswicks, and Cornelius Dewees. The latter was one of the charter members of the church, and served as Clerk of the church until his death in 1837. The only surviving members of the church are Miss Martha Cathel, her sister, Mrs. Mary B. Clifton, and a Mrs. Stettzer, who removed to the West years ago. Daniel Clifton, Esq., elected Trustee in 1839, is the only Trustee left. The old church-building, with its high pulpit, remains, and is occupied by an aged colored man and his family as a dwelling. Being a cripple, and living in the old church-building surrounded by graves and situated in a lonely place by the edge of the forest, he is dreaded, and regarded by those of his neighbors who are superstitious as a wizard.

Rev. E. Dazey and Rev. Joshua Dewees were Pastors of the church. The latter was born in the neighborhood, May 3, 1742. He was bred a Presbyterian, called to the ministry of this church, October 29, 1785, and ordained by Messrs. Fleeson, Boggs, and Dazey. "Mr. Dewees's transition from a state of nature to a state of grace," says Morgan Edwards (p. 272), "was tedious and distressing. His relation of that transition put me in mind of what John Bunyan saith of himself in his *Grace Abounding, etc.* But it will not be long before he makes another transit from a state of grace to a state of glory, for his lungs are ulcerated." The above Pastors were followed by Rev. Joseph Flood, who served the church for many years; Rev. S. Snead, 1804; Rev. Samuel Broadaway, from 1807 to 1809; and Rev. Peter Meredith.

8. Gravelly Branch Church, 1785.

The Gravelly Branch, Sussex County, was the seventh church organized through the ministry of Messrs. Baker and Hughes. When they had baptized about twenty-three converts they constituted them into a church, July 30, 1785. It entered the Salisbury Association the same year. A revival took place in this church in 1788, whereby thirty-five members were added to it. Messrs. Baker and Hughes, as was their custom with the churches they gathered, labored with this people for a while. Rev. Jonathan Gibbins then became Pastor, and in turn was succeeded by Rev. John Benson. The Pastor's salary was then (1791) forty pounds, or about two hundred dollars. They had no house, but worshipped in the dwelling of John Willis, "where," says Edwards (p. 267), "a movable pulpit stands." They were then preparing to build. They afterward built, but the church has ceased to exist. Though in early times some of these churches had no meeting-house, yet eventually each church succeeded in building one for its own accommodation.

9. The Bethel, built 1786; constituted 1839; dissolved 1872.

The Welsh Tract Church had out-stations, from which large accessions of members were received, "in the town of Elk," Maryland, and in New Castle County, Delaware, which latter they called Bethel, and where, in 1786, they built a house. The history of Bethel is somewhat interesting. David Morton, a Baptist, coming into New Castle County to live, invited Mr. Boggs, the Pastor, to preach at his house. The audience so increased that a private house would not hold them. "One day," says Mr. Edwards (p. 236), "as Mr. Boggs was preaching out of doors, a storm arose and dispersed the assembly. This induced two wealthy men present (Messrs. Porter and Louden) to talk of building a meeting-house in the place. The talk had at first the air of pleasantry, but ended in seriousness, and a house was built in 1786, measuring thirty-two feet by twenty-eight, and denominated Bethel." It was not, however, until 1839 that it was received as a church of sixteen members into the Delaware Association. We have no definite record, but it had probably just been constituted. After thirty-two years its name appears for the last time in the Minutes of the Delaware Association of 1871, with five members.

From the above it seems that Messrs. Baker and Hughes were instrumental in the formation of the Sounds, Broad Creek, Gravelly Branch, and Mispillion churches, but not directly in that of the Cow Marsh and Duck Creek. Nevertheless, I have included all under the head of their work, because their coming and labors led to the revival among the Baptists that resulted in the formation of all these churches and the raising up of a numerous and zealous ministry. The origin of the Baptists in Wilmington I shall consider under a separate head, though Mr. Hughes was one of those who labored successfully in that city.

The writer has not deemed it necessary up to this point to make material addition to what Edwards and Benedict have already furnished concerning these churches. They seem, however, at this point, destined to play an important part in the religious history of Delaware, and be great in number and influence, if they only continue as they have begun in the Missionary spirit and the aggressive labors that God ever blesses with success.

10. First Church, Wilmington, 1785.

This church was formed October 8, 1785. Their brick house of worship, thirty-five by forty feet, was built in the same year, and still stands. A graveyard surrounds the church. Says Morgan Edwards (pp. 273–275): "There were Baptists in Wilmington long before a Baptist Church existed in town; particularly Mrs. Ann Bush, a member of Welsh Tract Church; she settled here in 1748. In 1764, Mrs. Elizabeth Way, a member of Brandywine Church, came to the place. About 1769, Mr. John Stow, a member of Philadelphia Church, moved hither with his family. The residing of these Baptists in town induced Baptist ministers to preach here in a transient way, but they made no proselytes, insomuch that it was supposed that Wilmington was no soil to plant Baptists in. The first time that a prospect opened to the contrary was in 1782, when Rev. Philip Hughes came to print a volume of hymns. He preached here and gained some attention." In the month of April following (1783), Mr.

Thomas Ainger and family came from Philadelphia "to Wilmington Bridge." He was "a visible member" of Arch Street Presbyterian Church, Philadelphia, but his wife was a professed Baptist. And now, as Edwards says, "What Baptists could not do a Presbyterian did for them." It was mainly through him that a Baptist Church was established in Wilmington. This family invited Rev. Messrs. Fleeson and Boggs to preach at their house. "They complied, and serious impressions were made on the minds of the hearers. Mr. Fleeson judged it best to hold meetings in the town, which was done. And in the spring of 1784, Mr. Ainger and his family moved hither." "His family, including his apprentices, was then large, wherein he constantly held family worship, which consisted in reading the Bible, singing psalms, and prayers. One Sunday evening he read the twentieth chapter of Revelation, and found a strong impulse to comment upon it, particularly on the twelfth verse. This diffused a seriousness through the family, and laid a foundation for a religious society in which good was done. Two of his apprentices and some others attribute their conversion to this society. It quickened four more who had been converted previously. The converts were baptized by Rev. John Boggs, May 25, 1784. Their names were — Thomas Ainger, Rachel Ainger, Noah Cross, and Mrs. Ferris."

"The same year (1784) Rev. P. Hughes came to town to print his book on Baptism, which detained him near two months. He preached all the while, sometimes at Rev. Mr. McKannan's meeting-house, which still stands near the old Baptist meeting-house, and sometimes at the town school-house, which collected many hearers. By him were baptized four persons who had been awakened at said society—viz. Robert Smith, John Redman, James McLouchlan, Henry Walker." "Messrs. Fleeson and Boggs continued to visit the place alternately—viz. one each week. More were baptized by them, insomuch that a sufficient number of materials for a church were prepared at Wilmington." The candidates for baptism were baptized in the Brandywine. Some of those baptized—nine in number—had united with the Welsh Tract Church. These, obtaining letters of dismission for the purpose, were constituted, with six others, into a "gospel church,"

October 8, 1785, and united with the Philadelphia Association the next year. The council was composed of the following: Messrs. Fleeson and Boggs, Abel Griffiths, and Eliphaz Dazey. The constituent members, sixteen in number, were as follows: Thomas Ainger, James McLaughlin, Thomas Williams, Henry Walker, Joseph Tomlinson, John Redman, Robert Smith, John McKim, Curtis Gilbert, Sarah Stow, Elizabeth Hopkins, Mary Mattson, and four others who, it seems, were Baptists before this — John Stow, Elizabeth Way, Thomas Stow, and Abigail Ainger. Four of the constituent members became ministers —viz. Thomas Ainger, James McLaughlin, Henry Walker, and Curtis Gilbert. In five years this church increased to fifty-four members.

The publication of Rev. P. Hughes's book on Baptism in Wilmington, and the earnest preaching of believer's baptism by him and others, which led to the formation of the Baptist Church, aroused great opposition. The pulpits of two churches thundered against the Baptists and their principles, but there was one man, Father McKannan, Pastor of the

First Presbyterian Church, who acted wisely; he not only invited Mr. Hughes to preach for him, but this "veteran divine taught his audience to love their neighbors as themselves" (Edwards, 278). A few months ago (1879) the writer was present at the dedication of the new lecture-room of the First Presbyterian Church of Wilmington. The Pastor, Rev. B. F. Duval, pointed to some beautiful Corinthian columns that sustained the roof, remarking that they had adorned the old meeting-house, now used by the Historical Society of Delaware, when "Father McKannan" preached in it over one hundred years ago. When the writer's turn came to speak he did not fail to refer to the noble Christian charity of the "veteran divine" displayed upon the occasion mentioned.

Rev. Thomas Fleeson, Pastor of London Tract Church, was called for six months, and then for six months more, but regarding it as an unlimited call, removed with his family to Wilmington. He had been instrumental in gathering the church and building their house. He and Mr. Boggs not only preached for the church, but collected funds for the church-building. The first stone was laid by Mr. Fleeson, who made "an excellent prayer upon the occasion." "He saved a great part of his time to officiate to them (in connection with the church of which he was Pastor) between the constitution in 1785 and 1788, when one of their own members rose up to take pastoral charge of them—viz. Rev. Thomas Ainger" (Morgan Edwards, 273–275).

There are some particulars concerning the founder and Pastor of this church worth relating. Thomas Ainger was born in Philadelphia, May 12, 1755, bred a Presbyterian, baptized on profession of his faith and repentance, May 25, 1784, called to the ministry April 25, 1786, licensed May 19, 1787, and ordained by Rev. Messrs. Samuel Jones, David Jones, and Eliphaz Dazey, October 28, 1788, when he became Pastor of the church, in which office he continued until his death in 1797. He was buried in the churchyard, where his tomb remains. He had serious impressions made on his mind in early life, which wore off, but returned in manhood with more vigor and permanency. "He followed them to full communion in the Presbyterian Church, but was all the while a stranger to the liberty of the children of God." This liberty he obtained about the spring of 1780 from reading the eighth chapter of Romans, and particularly the first verse: "There is, therefore, now no condemnation to them which are in Christ." This he read with new eyes. His fears vanished, and confidence came in their place. He had frequent misgivings of heart in reference to the validity of infant baptism while a Presbyterian, which he strove to suppress, but happening to be on the banks of the Schuylkill when Baptism was administered, he saw it to be so conformable to gospel history that he resolved to go and do likewise. He administered the ordinance himself afterward in the same river. He was one of the council that recognized the Roxborough Church, and was the first Baptist minister (according to Rev. D. Spencer) to preach at Chestnut Hill, Philadelphia.

"For a few years after Mr. Ainger's death the church was supplied by the occasional labors of Mr. John Boggs, Sr., Gideon Farrell, John Ellis, and Joseph Flood. Mr. Flood did, indeed, exercise the pastoral care of it for a short time, when he was excluded for im-

DANIEL DODGE, D.D.

moral conduct—'for holding and preaching the doctrine of polygamy' (Minutes Delaware Association, 1803)—and afterward went to Norfolk, Virginia, and was the cause of much evil and confusion. But during the ministry of Mr. Flood, notwithstanding the blemishes of his character, and before they were known, there was a very considerable revival, and many were added to the church" (Benedict's *Abridged Baptist History*, p. 304). Thomas Ainger was Pastor till 1797. Five years later, Rev. Daniel Dodge came, whose long and successful pastorate of seventeen years terminated in his resignation in 1819. He baptized two hundred and fifty-nine converts while here. His influence was great for good while in Delaware, and he is held in loving remembrance by the people who knew him. There are but few such persons living, linking the present generation with the past; among these few is the venerable William Almond, father of the present Mayor of Wilmington. They love to recall the eloquence and zeal of this man of God. Often have they seen him come down from his high pulpit after preaching, singing an inspiring hymn and urging sinners to come to Christ. Mr. Dodge was born at Annapolis Royal, Nova Scotia, in 1775, but his father was a native of Ipswich, Massachusetts. Most of his time was spent in the United States. He professed conversion at the age of eighteen, and united with the church in Woodstock, Vermont, then under the charge of Elder Elisha Ransom. In 1797, he went to Baltimore, and preached in various places in Maryland and Virginia before he settled in Wilmington. He was ordained in 1801 in Anne Arundel County, Maryland. From Wilmington he went to Piscataway, New Jersey, where he was Pastor for thirteen years. He was Pastor next at Newark, New Jersey, for six years, and then of the Second Church, Philadelphia, from 1838 to 1850, following the Rev. T. J. Kitts in the pastorate of that church, with which he remained until his death. In 1839, he was elected Moderator of the Philadelphia Association. In 1812, while he was Pastor of the Wilmington Church, that church sought to withdraw from the Delaware Association, but was prevailed upon by the earnest solicitation of the Association to remain.

Rev. Samuel R. Green was Pastor from

1819* to 1824*. He was excluded from the church for dishonesty. Rev. David Lewis followed in 1824, and was Pastor to 1826.* Rev. John D. Strumpfer appears from the Minutes of the Association to have been Pastor in 1826* and 1827,* but some deny it. He was excluded. Rev. John P. Peckworth served the church from 1827* to 1838* with but a short intermission while he was in Alexandria. He was born in England in 1770, and came to Philadelphia at the age of thirteen. At seventeen he was baptized in Wilmington, and called to the ministry in the Philadelphia Church during the administration of Rev. Thomas Ustick. He was a constituent member of the Third Church, Philadelphia, and its first Pastor, serving from September, 1809, to December 20, 1822. He refused a salary of two hundred dollars from another church, preferring to serve the Third Church without pay, which he did three years, working at his trade, which was shoemaking, during the week, and preaching upon the Lord's Day. During his pastorate in Philadelphia he baptized two hundred and

* Dates taken from the Minutes of the Delaware Association.

thirty-seven and received by letter forty-six, and a meeting-house for the church was also erected. It is worthy of special note that during his pastorate the Sunday-school of the church took its rise. He was also Moderator of the Philadelphia Association. Those who followed Mr. Peckworth in the pastorate, as far as can be learned, are given here in the order of their service: John Miller, Alfred Earle, Joseph Smart, Wilson Housel, William Matthews, Samuel Earle, and Elder E. Rittenhouse, who came in 1858. Between the years 1846 and 1858 the Wilmington Church appears but seldom on the Minutes of the Delaware Association as sending either letter or messengers. For a part of this time the church was not in fellowship with the Association, and the name was dropped. Upon its reappearance it is put at the foot of the list. In 1862, the First Church applied to the Philadelphia Association for admission into that body, and being found to be in accord in faith and order with the Association by a Committee of which Rev. J. H. Kennard, D. D., was Chairman, was received and restored to its former place upon the roll. It remained until

1867, when the Philadelphia Association met in Wilmington with the Second Church. Then a Committee was appointed to consider the relation of the First Church to the Association. The Committee, Thomas Winter, D. D., Rev. W. H. H. Marsh, and Rev. G. W. Folwell, reported: That the male members of the church asserted that the application made in the name of the church for membership in the Philadelphia Association was made without sanction of the church proper, and that they were then, and continued to be, a member of another Association, from which they had no wish to be separated. The church was therefore dropped from the Minutes. In 1870, however, the church applied again, and was admitted into the Philadelphia Association. It is now, however, again a member of the Delaware Association.

11. Distinguished Men.

There were many ministers of note belonging to this period, who labored in the State or went thence to other fields of usefulness. The Thomases, Joneses, Griffiths, Davises, Suttons, Morgans, and Gibbinses were all known leaders in the Baptist denomination of their day. Some few of these princes in Israel, besides those already mentioned in these pages, are worthy of special consideration.

Rev. Jenkin Jones, though born in Wales in 1690, was called to the ministry in 1724 at Welsh Tract. He arrived in this country about 1710, and went to Philadelphia in 1725. He first had pastoral care of Lower Dublin and First Philadelphia churches jointly; but May 15, 1746, upon the reconstruction of the church in Philadelphia, he became Pastor of the latter only. He was the first Pastor that the First Church had wholly to itself, without dividing his time with others. He did real service to this church and to the interests of the Baptist denomination. He secured to the church their valuable lot and house, and was the moving cause of altering the direction of licenses, so as to enable dissenting ministers to perform marriage by them. "He built a parsonage-house, partly at his own charge. He gave a handsome legacy toward purchasing a silver cup for the Lord's Table which is worth upward of thirty pounds. His name is engraved upon it." He was Moderator of the Philadelphia

REV. ABEL MORGAN, A. M.

Association in 1756, and died in Philadelphia, July 16, 1760.

Abel Morgan, Jr., A. M., was born at Welsh Tract, April 18, 1713, and educated near by, at Pencader Academy, kept by Rev. Thomas Evans. He was ordained at Welsh Tract in 1734, and was called to the Middletown Church, New Jersey, which he served as Pastor till his death in the seventy-third year of his age. In 1772 he was Moderator of the Philadelphia Association, the celebrated Dr. James Manning being Clerk at the same time. Previously, Mr. Morgan served as Clerk. It was in 1774, upon his suggestion, that the Circular Letter was adopted by the Philadelphia Association for the first time. He was among the most noted Baptist ministers of his day. Dr. Samuel Jones calls him "the great, the incomparable Abel Morgan" (Benedict, p. 582). The same writer (p. 209) says: He "is the oldest writer I can find among the American Baptists in defence of their sentiments. Between this learned writer and Rev. Samuel Finley, a Presbyterian minister, then of Nottingham, Pennsylvania, a dispute appears to have arisen, which was carried on with much spirit on both sides for a number of years." "Mr. Finley was afterward President of Princeton College, New Jersey." "Mr. Morgan had the advantage," says Benedict in a note, "as a learned and logical debater." One of his works produced on this occasion—comprising one hundred and seventy-four pages—was printed in Philadelphia by the famous Benjamin Franklin in 1747, and though a small volume is valued now at fifteen dollars per copy. Previous to this Mr. Morgan had another controversy at Kingswood with Rev. Samuel Harker, also a Presbyterian minister.

Rev. John Davis, son of David Davis, Pastor of Welsh Tract, became Pastor of the Second Church, Boston, Massachusetts. He was a graduate of the University of Pennsylvania, and "a man of fine talents and of a finished education;" also "a truly pious man." He went to the church at Boston on trial in the spring of 1770, and in September following was ordained to the pastoral office. In less than two years he was compelled to resign on account of declining health, and shortly after died.

The Jones family have been distinguished in the annals of the Delaware Baptists. The most

P. 55.

prominent among them was Rev. David Jones, A. M. He was the son of Morgan and Eleanor (Evans) Jones, and born in White Clay Hundred, New Castle County, Delaware, May 12, 1736. He removed with his parents to Iron-hill in 1750, where he was brought to a saving knowledge of Christ in 1758, at the age of twenty-two, and baptized May 6, 1758, by Rev. David Davis, Pastor of the Welsh Tract Church. He studied under Rev. Isaac Eaton, A. M., at Hopewell, New Jersey, remaining three years, where he "learned Latin and Greek." In 1761, he became a licentiate of the Welsh Tract Church, and studied divinity at Middletown, New Jersey, under his kinsman, Rev. Abel Morgan, A. M. He was Pastor at Freehold, New Jersey, and at Southampton and Great Valley, Pennsylvania. He was the father of the late Rev. Horatio Gates Jones, D. D., and grandfather of Hon. H. G. Jones of Philadelphia.* Rev. David Spencer, in his *Early Baptists of Philadelphia*, says of him: "Rev. John Gano, in his letter to the First Baptist Church, as given in this chapter, speaks of popular men of character in the ministry that left the city,

* Sprague's *Annals*, vol. vi. p. 85.

and some in the State, to enter the chaplaincy of the country. One of these men certainly merits reference here—not that he was a Philadelphia Baptist, but as the ancestor of an honored family of our denomination in this city. Rev. David Jones is the gentleman spoken of. . . . Previous to the issuing of the Declaration of Independence he took high ground in favor of cutting loose from Great Britain. In 1776, he became a chaplain in the army, and remained through all the war, up to the surrender at Yorktown, performing very important service for his country. He was a man of warm friendship, ardent patriotism, and sincere piety, and after much faithful work for his Lord and Master he died February 5, 1824, in the eighty-fourth year of his age. He was buried in the graveyard of the Great Valley Baptist Church, near the very spot where, for many years as a Pastor, he preached the gospel of the blessed God" (pp. 128, 129).

Dr. William Cathcart, in his *Centennial Offering*, says: "The Rev. David Jones was an original thinker, and was fearless in expressing his sentiments. He was an educated man, but he possessed what schools never gave—a powerful intellect. As a preacher he always secured the undivided attention of his hearers, and never failed to instruct and cheer them. When the Revolutionary war began Mr. Jones lived in a section of New Jersey where Tories made it neither agreeable nor safe for a patriot to reside, especially if, like Mr. Jones, he was an orator capable of moving men by his eloquence, and a brave man to whom fear was an unexplored mystery. So Mr. Jones, believing that he could serve his country better than by martyrdom from such hands, removed to Pennsylvania. In 1775, on a public fast, he preached to the regiment of Col. Dewees a sermon overflowing with patriotism and with unshaken confidence in God. The discourse was given to the printer and widely circulated over the colonies, and it exerted an extensive influence in favor of the good cause. In 1776, Mr. Jones became chaplain of a Pennsylvania regiment, and entered upon duties for which he was better qualified than almost any other man among the patriotic ministers of America. He was never away from scenes of danger, nor from the rude couch of the sick or the wounded soldier when words of comfort were needed. He followed Gates through his campaigns, and served as a brigade chaplain under Wayne. He was in the battle of Brandywine, the slaughter of Paoli—where he escaped only by the special care of Providence—and in all the deadly conflicts in which his brigade was engaged until the surrender at Yorktown. Gen. Howe, learning that he was a pillar to the Revolution in and out of the army, offered a reward for his capture, and a plot was unsuccessfully laid to secure his person. Full of wit, eloquence, patriotism, and fearless courage, he was a model chaplain and a tower of strength to the cause of freedom. He was the grandfather of our esteemed brother, the Hon. Horatio Gates Jones of Pennsylvania" (pp. 38–40).

Conspicuous among the Baptist ministers who have made Delaware their home is Rev. Morgan Edwards, A. M., the well-known Baptist historian. Says Benedict: "He was emphatically a pioneer in the history of the Baptists." "For talents, industry, and usefulness," says the same writer, "he was pre-eminent in his day." He was a vigorous supporter of every Baptist enterprise of his day, and is justly regarded as the founder of Rhode Island College, now known as Brown University. He was born in Wales, May 9, 1722, and educated at the grammar-school at home and at Bristol Seminary. He entered the ministry at the age of sixteen. He was recommended to the First Church, Philadelphia, as Pastor, by the famous Dr. Gill of London and others, and became Pastor of that church in 1761. He resigned and moved to Newark, Delaware, in 1772, where he had purchased a farm. He continued to reside in the State until his death, at Pencader, New Castle County, on the 28th of January, 1795, in the seventy-third year of his age. He was buried, according to his request, in the aisle of the meeting-house in Philadelphia. During his twenty-three years' residence in Delaware he labored in the interests of Christ and of the denomination within and without the State. Up to the Revolution he continued preaching the word of life and salvation in a number of vacant churches. After the war he occasionally read lectures in divinity in Philadelphia and other parts of Pennsylvania, also in New Jersey, Delaware, and New England. His *Materials towards a History of the Baptists* of *Pennsylvania* were published in 1792, while he was in Delaware, and most of his materials toward the history of Baptists in other States were collected and written about the same time. For years he printed at his own expense annual tables showing the condition of the churches of the Philadelphia Association, and finally induced the Association to print its Minutes. He was at different times both Clerk and Moderator of that body. In 1762, Morgan Edwards was Moderator, and Abel Morgan Clerk. "They met at the Lutheran Church, in Fifth Street between Arch Street and Race Street, where the sound of the organ was heard in the Baptist worship." (See Minutes, 1762.) He was a man of extended travel and of pleasing manners. His Greek Testament, of which he was complete master, was his constant companion, while he loved his Hebrew Bible next. He called them the minister's two eyes. He was brought up an Episcopalian, and became a Baptist upon conviction. The large print-hand in which his *Manuscript Materials towards a Baptist History* is written can never be forgotten by those who have seen it.*

* Mr. Edwards was the only Baptist minister of that

JOSEPH H. KENNARD, D. D.

Rev. Thomas J. Kitts was ordained at the Wilmington Church in 1818, during the pastorate of Rev. Daniel Dodge. He was born in Pennsylvania, September 13, 1789. In 1818, he was Clerk of the Delaware Association. He was Pastor at the Great Valley in 1822, and became Pastor in 1823 of the Second Church, Philadelphia, which church he served until his death, January, 1838. He preached the sermon before the Philadelphia Association in 1826, and was Clerk in 1827, and Moderator in 1828. In character and preaching ability he was second to none.

Rev. Joseph H. Kennard, D. D., so well known to this generation, was converted under the ministry of Mr. Dodge, and baptized by him, July 3, 1814. He was also licensed to preach by the Wilmington Church, September, 1818. He was appointed, with others, by the Delaware Association in June, 1819, to represent them in the next Philadelphia Association, which was probably his first appearance as a delegate in the body of which he was so many years a leader. His first labors were as a mis-

day, so far as I can learn, who sympathized with the Loyalists.

sionary in this peninsula, "everywhere exciting attention by his youthfulness and glowing zeal." Mr. Kennard was born near Haddonfield, New Jersey, April 24, 1798, and his parents were Friends. He came to Wilmington when he was about fifteen years of age. He was called from his work in Delaware to the pastorate of the Baptist Church at Burlington, New Jersey, where he was ordained in July, 1820. He went in 1822 to the Second Church, Hopewell, New Jersey, and in October, 1822, to the Blockley Church, now in Philadelphia. While there he was largely instrumental in the formation of what is now the Pennsylvania General Association, of which he became the Missionary in 1830. In January, 1832, he accepted a call to become the Pastor of the New Market Street Church (now the Fourth), Philadelphia. His labors there were most successful. The house was crowded, souls were converted, and the church grew in numbers. Needing more room, nearly one hundred and seventy members went out and formed the Tenth Church, January 1, 1838, with Mr. Kennard as Pastor, which office he filled for the remainder of his life. This church reached a membership of eleven hundred during his pastorate, and was the mother of four or five vigorous churches. For a period of thirty-four years he was a settled Pastor in Philadelphia, and during his long life he baptized over two thousand persons. He was a man of great influence, not only in his own church and denomination, but other denominations, and the world acknowledged the power of his life for Christ. He died in the harness, Lord's Day evening, June 24, 1866, and was succeeded, according to the wish of his heart, by his son, Rev. J. Spencer Kennard, D. D.

Our brief mention of men of note in this connection would not be complete if the name of Captain Calvin Tubbs were omitted. It is impossible to find out much about him, but enough is known to make his name conspicuous in Baptist history. He was a native of New England, a sea-captain by occupation, and lived for many years when ashore in Newark, Delaware, or on his farm at Aikenville in the same State. He married Mary, the daughter of Rev. Gideon Farrell, who was Pastor of Welsh Tract Church from 1802 to 1820. Mr. William M. Campbell, Clerk of that church, sends me the following, taken from the Minutes: "May 27, 1815, yearly meeting. The Association being held on the first Sabbath in June, which is the day of our monthly meeting, the church was now called together to attend to business. 1st. Captain Calvin Tubbs came forward and offered his experience with a view to be baptized and join the church. He was accordingly received for baptism, to be performed on the morrow morning." "He was present to appointment, and was baptized and received a member at Bethel meeting on the second Sabbath in June at the quarterly meeting." The latter words are probably those of Mr. Campbell, condensed from the record. An old member of the Welsh Tract, now living, informs me that he was present and saw Captain Tubbs baptized. Being "yearly meeting," it was performed in the presence of a large concourse of people. Bethel was a mission of Welsh Tract. Captain Tubbs in 1830 united with the Fifth Baptist Church, as Rev. B. D. Thomas, Pastor, tells me. It was then the Sansom Street Church, Philadelphia. He was a member there for only a short time. He and his wife and children are buried in the graveyard of the Welsh Tract

J. G. ONCKEN, D. D.

Church, in the rear of the house. He was a godly man, and is well remembered by many now living in Philadelphia, as well as in Delaware. Says Captain Turley: "He flew the Bethel flag on Sunday."

It is, however, chiefly of his connection with the conversion to Baptist views of the great German apostle, Rev. John G. Oncken, D. D., that I wish to speak. This matter was first brought to the attention of the writer by Miss Anne Semple of Wilmington, Delaware, who knew him well and played with his children. Miss Semple says: " Captain Tubbs commanded a vessel sailing between Philadelphia and Hamburg, belonging to the late John Welsh, Esq., of Philadelphia, whose wife was a member of Sansom Street Baptist Church, and who was the father of the ex-Minister to England. One winter his vessel was providentially ice-bound at Hamburg, and he boarded in the city. In the same house was a young man, a colporteur from London, named J. G. Oncken, a Pedobaptist. They became intimate, and among other religious subjects discussed interchanged their views on the ordinance of Baptism. Mr. Oncken, being convinced that the captain had the Bible on his side, and consequently that he was not baptized, requested that on his return home he would make his case known to some Baptist minister going to Europe, and ask him to visit Hamburg and baptize him."

In Lehmann's *History of the Baptist Churches in Germany*, etc., translated by G. Anderson, D. D. (p. 5), we read: "Finally, *after many years*, Dr. Barnas Sears of America, who now occupies a high position in the United States, came to Hamburg, entered into intimate relations with Oncken, and was thus prepared to administer baptism to him and to the few believers who found themselves in fellowship with Oncken, and shared his convictions in respect to the ordinances. It was on the 22d of April, 1834, that the above-mentioned solemn baptism was administered to him and to six others, and thus was laid the foundation of the first Baptist Church in Hamburg and in Germany. The event caused a great sensation wherever Oncken's name was known. On account of his meetings and preaching he had already suffered persecution, which now rose to an unusual height."

The following letters explain themselves:

From the Hon. John Welsh, ex-Minister of the United States to England.

MY DEAR SIR:

I am sorry that I am unable to give you the information you wish to get in regard to the late Captain Tubbs. We have no knowledge of his son Calvin, but my brother says he had a son called after him, Samuel Welsh Tubbs, who some years ago was in New York, but he knows nothing of his present residence, not having heard of him for several years.

Very respectfully,

JOHN WELSH.

PHILADELPHIA, May 10, 1880.
REV. R. B. COOK.

It was in hopes of finding something of the nativity of Captain Tubbs from the registers of the Welsh firm that the letter to which the above is the reply was written.

From Rev. P. W. Bickel, D. D.

HAMBURG, den 6 April, 1880.

REV. RICH. B. COOK, *Wilmington, Del.*

DEAR BROTHER:

Your favor of the 9th March has just come to hand. I went over to Mr. Oncken, and tried to get the information desired. Mr. Oncken remembered his good Captain Calvin Tubbs very well, and spoke of him with tenderest regard, but as to my question, Whether he was a Baptist when he first met the captain? he could give me no definite answer. He only said, "I think I was no Baptist yet, but my memory is so poor that I cannot give you any certainty."

Am sorry I cannot give you a better report. Mr. Oncken's memory is so weak that no reliance can be put in it now.

May God bless you in your work and multiply his people in every land and among every tribe!

Yours fraternally,
Philipp W. Bickel.

From Rev. Barnas Sears, D. D., LL.D.

Staunton, Va., April 29, 1880.

Rev. R. B. Cook.

Dear Brother:

I often heard Mr. Oncken speak of Captain Tubbs, who was, I think, at different times at Hamburg, and with whom Mr. Oncken corresponded. He always spoke of him with the greatest Christian affection. My *impression* is that Mr. Oncken got his Baptist views first from him; that is, that he first *talked* with him on the subject of Baptism. His own doubts may have preceded that time. As Secretary of the Lower Saxony Tract Society he expressed his doubts in a letter to Dr. Maclay, and Dr. Maclay asked me to seek him out in Hamburg, which I did, and I found his views settled on the subject. He wished me to converse with his wife and four or five others, who were then much troubled with doubts; all of whom were baptized afterward.

Yours truly,
B. Sears.

From John L. Dagg, D. D.

HAYNESVILLE, Ala., August 28, 1880.

REV. R. B. COOK.

DEAR BROTHER:

Your letter of the 17th inst. was received yesterday. . . . Brother Calvin Tubbs was a highly-esteemed member of the Fifth Baptist in Philadelphia when I was its Pastor. The place of his nativity I cannot tell you. His wife was a daughter of a Baptist minister in the State of Delaware. . . . I think it was Gideon Farrell. Brother Tubbs was captain of a trading vessel which used to sail from Philadelphia to Hamburg. At Hamburg he formed acquaintance with the Rev. J. G. Oncken while yet a Pedobaptist, and not only became much interested in him, but interested me also by the account of him which he gave me. At one time he showed me a letter which he had received from him, and which at my request he permitted me to get published. It was published in the *Baptist Tract Magazine*, the organ of the American Baptist Publication Society, and this published letter, I think, was the first thing that brought Mr. Oncken to the notice of our American people. . . . On the question whether Captain Tubbs had any connection with the conversion of Mr. Oncken to Baptist views I can say nothing. . . .

Your brother in Christ,

J. L. DAGG.

From Jonah G. Warren, D. D.
NEWTON CENTRE, Mass., August 12, 1880.

REV. R. B. COOK.

MY DEAR BROTHER:

Yours of the 11th is at hand. In looking into my copy-book, containing letters written from Germany in 1867, I find the following reference to Captain Tubbs. It occurs in a description I gave of a certain house in which Oncken at one time lived, and reads thus:

"While living in this house, an American seaman, Captain Tubbs, a member of the old Sansom Street Baptist Church, Philadelphia, being ice-bound, was compelled to spend the winter in Hamburg. Oncken took him into his family, and during the long winter evenings they talked over the doctrines and practices of the Baptist churches in the United States, prayed together, and together went to the 'upper room' and worshipped God in company with the band of believers. When he returned home Captain Tubbs told his Pastor, Mr. Dagg, and afterward Dr. Cone, what a treasure he had found in Hamburg, and how his late 'host' was looking for some one to baptize him. God always has some way to bring to pass his grand designs. Soon after correspondence was opened between America and Germany, and results whose fame is in all the churches followed in rapid succession."

I may say, in addition, that my book, now open before me, gives the fullest, most accurate and detailed description I have ever seen of the origin and progress of the Baptist work in Germany as connected with

Oncken, and I believe the best in existence, as it was taken down on the spot from Dr. Oncken's own lips. . . .

Yours most truly,
J. G. WARREN.

Enough has been said to show that German Baptists, if not Germany, are under obligation to Captain Tubbs, a missionary Baptist of the Welsh Tract Church, and through him to the Baptists of "Little Delaware." The blessing has already returned to us, for Jeremiah Grimmell, the founder of the German Church in Wilmington, was baptized by Dr. Oncken. It gives us a peculiar pleasure to begin the history of the great German Baptist movement, so far-reaching and wonderful, upon Delaware soil. Dr. Oncken acknowledges his indebtedness in the following extract from a letter acknowledging the reception of tracts from the American Baptist Publication Society, contained in the *Tract Magazine* for 1833: "The publications of your Society on Baptism are admirable. They were quite new to me, and have tended not a little to establish me in my purpose to comply with this part of my Saviour's command as soon as possible."*

* For those who wish to examine the matter further I

In the days of these men the Baptists of Delaware were a missionary, and consequently a growing, people, and Delaware was a centre of Baptist power and influence. Here is an extract illustrative of the missionary spirit of this period, taken from the Corresponding Letter of the Delaware Association, written by John M. Peck and endorsed by Rev. Jethro Johnson, Moderator, and approved by the Association at the meetings the year following that in which Captain Tubbs was baptized (1816): "If we take a cursory view of what has been effected in the last twenty-five years, who can withhold the exclamation, '*What hath God wrought!*' At that period the missionary flame commenced in Europe: it hath kindled across continents and islands, until the same holy fervor, in a good degree, warms the hearts of God's children on every side of the globe. No difficulties are insuperable to the zeal which animates the heralds of salvation: they go forth in every direction, bearing the precious treasure of

---

refer them to *The Baptist Missionary Magazine* for 1834 (p. 290), 1835 (p. 229), 1836 (p. 223), 1837 (p. 65), 1838 (p. 229). The Rev. Frank S. Dobbins has kindly furnished me with these references.

eternal life. Already the streams of salvation are poured upon the burning plains of India! The disciples of Brahma, the votaries of Juggernaut, and the deluded followers of the Arabian impostor catch the song of redeeming love! Ethiopia is beginning to stretch forth her hands to God, and the isles to wait for his law! . . . The real Christian, while viewing, on the one hand, the darkness, misery, and guilt of a large portion of the human family who are famishing for the '*bread of eternal life,*' and on the other the ardent zeal discovered to relieve their miserable state, pants for the privilege of entering into the harvest. . . . Had we lived half a century ago, we might have been suffered to sleep securely, insensible to the wants of our perishing fellow-men. . . . Let us cast our eyes on the multitudes around us in this land of gospel light, . . . without the means of religious instruction. . . . Let us feel for the poor Hindoo. . . . Let us be aroused by these considerations to make one united and vigorous effort to spread the gospel of Jesus both at home and abroad."

12. THE DELAWARE ASSOCIATION, 1795.

Benedict says that an Association was formed among the Baptists of Delaware, but at what date he is unable to say. It seems from the following, published in 1830, that the date of organization was 1795: "The Constitution of the Delaware Baptist Association, ratified and confirmed by the delegates of the Welsh Tract, Cow Marsh, Duck Creek, Queen Anne's, Wilmington, and Mispillion churches, the 24th day of October, A. D. 1795." This document is signed by the Pastors of the churches at that time, and by one delegate from each church. Other proof is not wanting. Five of these churches were in Delaware, and one probably in Maryland. Several churches in Pennsylvania soon joined the Association, those of them connected with the Philadelphia Association withdrawing for the purpose. According to the Minutes of the Philadelphia Association of 1794, the Cow Marsh, Welsh Tract, Duck Creek, and Wilmington churches requested "approbation and dismission" from the Association "to join another." It was voted that as the relation had been a long and happy one, they would be glad to have it continue; but if they wished to withdraw, consent was granted. They withdrew, and formed the Delaware Association, as we have seen. One, the Mispillion, came from the Salisbury Association. It seems, then, that union between Delaware and Pennsylvania churches in a Delaware Association is no new thing. Benedict says that the Delaware Association was a corresponding body of the Philadelphia Association as early as 1798, but the Philadelphia Association sent both letter and messenger to them in 1796, which was the first meeting held after the organization. At the same meeting of the Philadelphia Association, Dr. Rogers and Rev. T. Ustick were appointed to revise and publish the materials toward a history of the Baptists in Delaware by Morgan Edwards, just dead. Of the four churches in Delaware that had joined the Salisbury Association, three—viz. the Sounds, Broad Creek, and Gravelly Branch—continued in that connection. All the other Baptist churches in Delaware united with the new Association.

The Delaware Association was composed—
In 1801 of 5 churches and 293 members.
" 1825 " 9 " " 596 "
" 1879 " 7 " " 197. "

Four of the seven churches reported in 1879 are in Delaware, and with a total membership of one hundred and twenty-eight. There are besides two churches in the Salisbury Association, Little Creek and Broad Creek, with seventy-two members, in all (Salisbury Min. of 1879) making a total in the State, belonging to these six churches, of two hundred members. The once-flourishing Welsh Tract Church has decreased from one hundred and ninety-two in 1817 to sixty-four in 1879, while in the same period the First Wilmington has fallen from two hundred and eight to eleven. And this decline does not come because the new churches established draw from them, for only one new interest has been established by the efforts of the earlier churches of the Delaware Association since 1786, or for nearly a century. One church has been organized in that time, for which I cheerfully give them all the credit due. It is called the Bethel, and was started in 1786 as a mission in New Castle County by the Welsh Tract Church. It was made to stand alone by its mother in 1839, and constituted a church with sixteen members after an existence as a mission of forty-six years. There were also three churches formed in the lower part of the State in the early part of this century, and connected with the Salisbury Association—the Bethel, in Sussex County, the Little Creek, and the Millsborough. The Little Creek is the only one of the three that survives, and is served in conjunction with the Broad Creek Church by Elder E. Rittenhouse, who is Pastor also of the First Wilmington Church, *and the only Pastor of the Old School denomination now (1880) in the State.* The Gravelly Branch, Sounds, Mispillion, Bethel in New Castle County, Bethel in Sussex County, and Millsborough churches are no more; their light has gone out, their "candlestick" has been removed, and their empty meeting-houses stand like deserted windmills, testifying of the industry of a past age that built them, and of the progressive spirit of the present that has left them far behind. And "the things which remain" "are ready to die." The most indication of life is observable in the venerable Welsh Tract Church. Yet even here regular service is held only twice a month, while with the others it is but monthly. The attendance at all of them is mostly small.

The meetings of the Association, which are annual, are sometimes largely attended.

The cause of this unusual decline in our denominational affairs, and of the decayed and feeble state of these early churches, is thus stated by Rev. Morgan J. Rhees, then of Delaware, himself a Welshman, in Benedict's *History of the Baptists:* "One general remark is true of them all: '*They progress backward.*' There has been a regular decline for years, even greater than is exhibited by their returns and their congregations, to *almost nothing.* There is one prominent reason why these churches, and those of a kindred spirit in Delaware and Maryland and everywhere else, are declining, and do not and cannot prosper. You will find it in Haggai i. 2–12 and in Malachi iii. 8–11. They withhold from the Lord's cause that which he demands, and the result is the heavens withhold their blessings. God has called for a drought upon them in spiritual things, and they are withering and fast decaying; and it needs no prophetic gift to see their speedy dissolution unless they repent and return to the Lord and engage in his service. It is lamentable to see the light extinguished where it shone so clearly, but it is in accordance with his plans who doeth all things well, and who will be honored by the service of his professed disciples. These churches opposed all missionary, Bible, Sunday-school, tract, and temperance organizations, and are thus hindering the fulfilment of the Saviour's command 'to preach the gospel in all the world, to every creature,' as far as they can do it; and while they thus act they cannot prosper" (p. 630).

They are numerically much weaker to-day than when these words were written (1845), and we can almost hear the Saviour say to them, as to the church at Sardis: "FOR I have not found thy *works* perfect before God." Were these always the principles and practices of these churches? we ask. Their history before the formation of the Delaware Association, the multiplication of members and churches among them through their own missionary labors as well as those of others, prove that their faith and practice have changed. And for a quarter of a century after the formation of the Delaware Association these were missionary churches, favoring societies for extending the Redeemer's kingdom at home and in foreign lands. But first let us hear the testimony of the fathers upon these points.

Benedict, in his *History of the Baptists* (p. 626), says: "The numbers and influence of the denomination in this State for many years was small, yet it was for a long time equal, in proportion to the population, to any of the Middle States." "The community at Welsh Tract in early times held a respectable stand among the American Baptists; it was one of the five churches which formed the Philadelphia Association; its ministers were among the most active in all Baptist operations; and the whole concern was not behind any of the members of that quintuple alliance." A. D. Gillette, D. D., in the Centenary volume of the Philadelphia Association Minutes (p. 15, 1849), says: "This church appears to be very regular in its first settlement, and hath been the best supplied with ministers of any church belonging to this Association." W. Cathcart, D. D., in his *Centennial Offering* (p. 62), says that "John Adams of Massachusetts was on some occasions the bitterest enemy of the Baptists in Revolutionary days, and yet he gives them considerable credit for bringing Delaware from the gulf of disloyalty, to the brink of which, he declares 'the missionaries of the London Society for the Propagation of the Faith in Foreign Parts' had brought her, to the platform of patriotism."* This shows their influence at an early date. In 1790, M. Edwards writes (p. 224 *MS. History of Delaware*): "The Delaware Baptists are *Calvinistic* in doctrine, and differ little or nothing in discipline from their brethren in neighboring States."

From these extracts it appears that they were strong, influential, patriotic, and orthodox as to faith and practice.

Still later, Benedict says of all the Delaware Baptist churches, that they "were in full fellowship and cordial co-operation with their brethren in all plans of benevolence and evangelical efforts, and their course was prosperous and progressive" (p. 30).

Let us now follow briefly the history of the early Baptists, as we find it in the Minutes of their own Association, the Delaware. We shall find that the latter statement of Benedict is strictly true in every particular. In 1804, they were a missionary people, for they pro-

* *Life and Works of John Adams*, by Charles Francis Adams, x. p. 812.

vided for a missionary sermon and a collection in each church for the support of "missionary brethren" preaching the gospel in destitute places. In 1812, a plan of the "Baptist Education Society for the Middle States" was read and approved. This was doubtless a society for ministerial education, to which they are now opposed. When the Foreign Mission Society of the Baptist denomination in America, now known as the American Baptist Missionary Union, was organized in Philadelphia, May 18, 1814, by thirty-three delegates from all parts of the country, two of this number were ministers closely identified with Delaware—namely, Rev. John P. Peckworth, then Pastor in Philadelphia, and Rev. Daniel Dodge, Pastor in Wilmington and the representative from Delaware in the body. In June following (1814) the Delaware Association passed the following: "This Association having learned with pleasure that a general Board of Commissioners for Foreign Missions has been formed in the city of Philadelphia, whose object is to translate the Scriptures into the different languages of the heathen and send the gospel among them, we do therefore recommend to our brethren and friends to encourage the Missionary Society formed in this State."

This action endorses missions and missionary societies, and shows the existence of an auxiliary society in Delaware.

In the record of 1815 we find the following minute: "It is with heartfelt satisfaction we have received communications from our Brother Rice, with the first Report of the Board of Foreign Missions, accompanied with a letter from their Corresponding Secretary, and would earnestly recommend to our brethren to have a missionary sermon preached annually in their respective churches, and a collection raised and forwarded to the branch society of Delaware."

In 1816, at Welsh Tract, the Association passed the following: "It is with pleasure that we have received the following letter from the Corresponding Secretary of the Baptist Board of Foreign Missions (Dr. Staughton), with a request that it be inserted in our minutes, and have appointed Brother Dodge as our Corresponding Secretary to receive and distribute the next Annual Report (the second) of the Board, and preserve our correspondence with them." The letter referred to is printed in full in the Minutes.

At the same meeting the first Report of the Delaware Bible Society was presented and affectionately commended to the brethren. At this time (1816) the Welsh Tract Church had a membership of one hundred and ninety, and the Wilmington Church two hundred and eight. This shows the effect of the missionary spirit. Now (1879) the Welsh Tract numbers but sixty-four, and the Wilmington Church only eleven.

In 1817, the Constitution of "The Delaware Society for Domestic Missions" was adopted by the Association, and printed in the Minutes. Its object was to "aid poor and destitute churches in the support of the stated ministry of the word, and to supply destitute neighborhoods with the gospel." The Society existed for years, carried out its object, met with and had its proceedings printed in the Minutes of the Association. Women were appointed collectors in all the churches.

In 1818, Rev. Samuel R. Green, Pastor of the First Wilmington Church, wrote in the Corresponding Letter: "Although there are not many added to our little number to swell our song of praise, yet the pleasure of hearing that our churches are firmly established in the faith, and that they are cemented in love, cheers our hearts. The kingdom of the Lord is rapidly advancing; the stone cut out of the mountains without hands is spreading; the little handful of corn that is scattered upon the mountains shall wax like Lebanon. Christians are uniting their energies; the gospel is spreading. . . . Ethiopia is about to stretch forth her hands unto God. We live in an eventful period. Much remains to be done. May we, brethren, look about us, and while we pray *Thy kingdom come,* endeavor to exert every nerve, remembering that God has connected the means with the ends."

In 1820, the Association " Resolved, That our Brother David Greene be appointed our missionary, as far as our funds will admit, and that he be authorized to make collections as often as expedient, whenever he may preach, to aid the funds of this Society. That Brother Greene, receive four dollars per week for his services, and that he have a letter of recommendation, signed by the Moderator and Clerk of this Association." In the Corresponding Letter of the same year Rev. Jethro Johnson says: "It appears by the information we received during the session from different parts of the continent that a union in sentiment and practice generally prevails among our churches, and that although additions are not numerous, yet peace almost universally prevails, and most of the meeting-houses among us are commonly crowded with attentive hearers. The gradual increase of the gospel, together with the missionary spirit that in almost every place appears to prevail, leads us to believe that prophecies are actually fulfilling 'Thy kingdom come.'"

In the Corresponding Letter of 1822, they say: "The accounts we have had from different sources, and especially from the Mission Board, are truly refreshing." ... "May we feel ourselves deeply interested in this, and esteem it not only our duty to put up our prayers, but to use *all* the means God has placed in our power, believing at the same time that he who hath said, 'He must increase,' hath also declared, 'Be ye workers together with God.'"

One might suppose from this that there were differences of opinion among them, but in 1824 the Corresponding Letter says: "We have the pleasure to inform you that harmony now prevails in our churches." Also, "We have been cheered with accounts from various parts of the world, in which the Lord is lifting up his banner and drawing souls to it, and we earnestly pray that he will continue to display the powers of his grace."

In 1825, they received a report from the "Baptist General Tract Society," now the "American Baptist Publication Society," through the agent in Wilmington, Samuel Harker. It was referred for examination to Messrs. Dale and Woolford, who reported, highly approving its design and wishing encouragement for it; and this report was adopted. At the same meeting the formation of a Domestic Mission Society was recommended, and it was agreed that a special meeting take place for the purpose at Bethel; that a missionary sermon be preached by either Jethro Johnson or Thomas Barton; that an appeal for aid be made in an address; and that a certain constitution be adopted to carry the purpose into immediate effect, so far as to proceed in obtaining subscribers.

We append a few extracts from the address,

prepared by Messrs. Barton and Woolford, and published in the Minutes and endorsed by the Association: "Upon our Peninsula there has been, and still remains to be, a lamentable deficiency in the supply of the preaching of the gospel. The Christian, . . . realizing . . . the danger to which the unconverted soul is exposed, . . . is disposed to employ his purse and his pen that he may aid in disseminating a knowledge of that only 'name given under heaven among men, whereby we must be saved.' The ordinary means by which this knowledge is to be obtained is the preaching of the gospel. . . . We are called upon by the most imposing considerations to regard the condition of those who are famishing for want of the water of life, and to endeavor to supply them. . . . Those who can be indifferent . . . are certainly not under the proper influence of the spirit which the religion of the cross is calculated to produce."

The next year (1826) the Corresponding Letter says: "Since our last communication we have formed a Society for Domestic Missions, to carry the word of life into those places adjacent on this Peninsula which are destitute; and we trust that the zeal and vigor with which the thing is entered into is an indication that the time to favor Zion is at hand."

The record in 1827 is: "No questions gendering strife have interrupted the harmony of our present meeting;" while the next year their session was "particularly harmonious;" and they were greatly rejoiced in communicating "the pleasing intelligence of *large additions to our churches.*"

In 1830, the Association, by the unanimous approval of the churches, ordered to be printed the Constitution and Rules before referred to as having been previously adopted in 1795, and signed by the ministers and delegates of the churches at that time. This shows that their faith in 1830 was the same as in 1795. This document is preserved with their Minutes.

But notice the final article of faith: "Finally, we approve of the Confession of Faith adopted by the Philadelphia Association, September 25, 1742, as generally expressing our opinion of the Holy Scriptures, which we hold above all as the only certain rule of faith and practice." This carries us back fifty-three years more, and we find the doctrines of 1742 unchanged in 1830, and in accord with the Philadelphia Association. And in this same year (1830) we find them in fellowship and corresponding with the Philadelphia, Hudson River, New York, and New Jersey Associations, and receiving by vote the Central New Jersey Association as a corresponding body.

From the foregoing facts we are justified in reaffirming that the earlier and the later missionary Baptist churches of Delaware are one; but from this period on, mark the change.

Rev. Samuel Trott became Pastor of Welsh Tract Church in 1831, and immediately appears to have taken the front in leading the churches away from the faith. In the Corresponding Letter of 1831 he says: "We receive him (Christ) as our Pattern; hence we do not walk in the observance of many things which have been introduced among Baptists generally, and received, though of human contrivance, as of great importance in furthering the cause of religion, because we do not see our Jesus going before in the practice of them, and we desire to keep in his footsteps, believing it the safest path. Hence we prefer praying to him, the Lord of the harvest, to send forth laborers into his harvest such as he shall choose and qualify, and rely on his wisdom, power, and faithfulness to provide all things necessary for gathering in his elect and extending the knowledge of his salvation to the ends of the earth, to resorting to the plans of human contrivance, however plausible, for accomplishing these things." In 1832, he returns to the charge in the Circular Letter endorsed by the Association, and condemns the plan of ministerial support by salaries, the mission societies (ministers-agents, missionaries of societies), and theological seminaries.

In the Corresponding Letter of the same year, Rev. Thomas Barton says: "Our letters chiefly complain of small ingatherings. . . . As to the cause of the state of our churches, various conjectures exist. By one, lamentable inertness and the predominancy of anti-effort principles is assigned as the cause. As to the first, we hope none of us are prepared to adopt the invitation of Jehu, 'Come, see my zeal for the Lord of hosts,' but with humility would acknowledge our shortcomings. As to the modern system, imposed upon the churches under the *assumed* authority of divine institutions, we are not prepared to receive it. We know that the work of salvation is of God; and why he does not convert more sinners among us we leave to him," etc.

After 1834 the Philadelphia Association is dropped from the Minutes as a corresponding body, the New York, Hudson River, New Jersey, Central New Jersey, and other Associations having been dropped before.

The crisis, however, came in 1835, when a handful of faithful ones withdrew from the church at Wilmington and formed the Second Church.

Rev. William K. Robinson, Pastor of Welsh Tract Church, writes in the Corresponding Letter of 1835: "We have truly reason to lament the state of things, while there are so many that have embraced the general system of doctrine and the whole brood of benevolent institutions so called, therein uniting the church and the world together, saying that in money there is power sufficient, if there can be enough obtained, to save the whole world; but we as an Association have not so learned Christ." And in 1836 the Association refused by vote to receive into fellowship persons baptized " by those who are engaged in the new-fangled systems of the day." In the same year (1836) the Corresponding Letter, written by one "Brother Scott," and signed by Rev. Peter Meredith, Pastor at Cow Marsh, as Moderator of the Association, contains the following: "Jesus Christ has been set forth as the only way of life and salvation, and that entirely independent of human agency. The enemy has made a descent upon one of our churches to sow the seeds of discord, and by that means endeavor to carry off the prize; but in this we rejoice to say that they have been disappointed and their partial triumphs have proved a blessing to us."

It proved their ruin and a blessing to the cause of Christ, for while they have dwindled to eleven, the thirteen who seceded now number in Wilmington alone five churches and fifteen hundred and eighty-six members.

"We are," he continues, "but a feeble body, and much exposed to the innovations of the learned gentry of the day, who swarm out of the theological institutions like locusts, and are ready to devour the land." What would the writer say now to see so many noble young men trained at the Crozer Theological Seminary laboring in Delaware in the cause of Christ?

The misrepresentations and unfairness of some of these statements as to the doctrines and practices of missionary Baptists are apparent to every well-informed mind. It is, doubtless, the case that the Antinomianism that led to the separation of 1835, as well as the change of action in the Association, was for some time gathering force, like a smouldering fire, before it gained controlling power.

The Corresponding Letter of the Philadelphia Association of 1834 contains the following words, which show plainly the wide difference then and now existing between those calling themselves the Old School Baptists and those called the New School: "Our churches generally are rooted and grounded in the faith, and in *that* faith which is fruitful of good works. The circulation of the Holy Scriptures and of evangelical tracts; the teaching of sacred truth to our children in Sunday-schools; the promotion of temperance associations, with kindred institutions, having in view the glory of God and the advancement of the best interests of our fellow-men—have enlisted, and are continuing to enlist more and more, the affections and the energies of our body."

In 1856, for the first time, the Association is called in the Minutes the "Delaware *Old School* Baptist Association." The school to which they belong is doubtless old. Do-nothings need not search far for precedents and ancestors even among Baptists. But, had they chosen to do so, they could have discovered Baptists in unbroken line whose labors and successes render *them* worthy of emulation by all who come after them, and especially by those who glory in the Baptist name, which their lives have made honorable as the very synonym of Christian activity.

Who the men were that led the churches away from the faith and practice of the fathers is apparent in some cases. Some of them were ministers of the Delaware Association and Pastors of the Baptist churches connected with it in Pennsylvania and Delaware. Some of them at one time were active in the cause of Christ and of missions. We have brought together in these pages their views and actions at different times, and found them to be in strong contrast. They changed, and the churches and the Association changed with them. One notable instance is that of the Rev. Philip Hughes, who, after laboring so zealously in the cause of missions, embraced Antinomian views, and thus became widely separated from his former companion in labor, Mr. Baker. His name is merely mentioned by Semple, and not at all by Taylor, and the reason is given in Semple's *History* (p. 397, note): He became intemperate in habit as well as Antinomian in view. "His last days were a blot upon his first." He died at Dr. Lemon's, where Mr. Baker had ended his days so gloriously. I would not doubt the piety and good intentions of these men, but results prove that theirs were fatal mistakes—fatal to the very life and existence of the churches that they meant to serve. Would that their churches would own their error, retrace their steps, and help to recover, in part at least, what has been lost!

II.—THE LATER BAPTIST CHURCHES.

1. THE SECOND CHURCH, WILMINGTON, 1835.

The first of these was the Second Church, Wilmington, organized September 7, 1835,

SECOND CHURCH, WILMINGTON.

P. 96.

with thirteen members, dismissed by request from the First Church. Being opposed to the erroneous views and practices into which the latter had fallen, they separated to form a missionary church. The constituent members were Gideon F. Tindall, Susanna Boulden, John Heazlet, Susan Darby, Moses Bannister, Ann Bannister, Robinson Beckley, Margaret Springer, Sally Ann Todd, Sarah A. Graham, Margaret Sterrett, Mary E. Stroud, and Jane Cochran. Of these but three are living: Gideon F. Tindall, Robinson Beckley, and Mary E. Stroud.

The Council by which the church was constituted was composed of the following ministers: Rev. Joseph H. Kennard and Rev. James J. Woolsey of Philadelphia, Rev. Leonard Fletcher of Great Valley, Pa., and Rev. George I. Miles of West Chester, Pa. It will be observed that this movement received recognition from Pennsylvania, and that no Delaware minister was present. The next year (1836) the church united with the Philadelphia Association. The American Baptist Home Mission Society extended aid to this feeble band at this time and once afterward.

The new church worshipped first in a rented room on Sixth Street, and in the old meeting-house of the First Presbyterian Church. They soon secured a house of their own, on the corner of Walnut and Fifth Streets, now occupied by the German Baptist Church. During the eighteen years they occupied this house great prosperity attended them. For seven years of this period Rev. Morgan J. Rhees, D. D., was their Pastor, during whose pastorate the church reached a membership of four hundred, and showed great liberality in their contributions to the various objects of benevolence. One year they report one thousand dollars contributed for benevolence abroad. Besides, they became self-sustaining, giving up voluntarily the aid extended to them by the American Baptist Home Mission Society. In 1848, while Pastor here, Dr. Rhees was made Moderator of the Philadelphia Association.

In 1852, Rev. Frederick Charlton being Pastor, the church resolved to build in a new location, and Mr. Washington Jones was made Chairman of the Building Committee. A lot was purchased at the corner of Fourth and French Streets, and the present commodious

WASHINGTON JONES.

WM. G. JONES.

house of worship built. It will seat over six hundred persons, and is worth at least thirty thousand dollars. Mr. Jones took an active part in the enterprise, both by his own large contributions and his zealous efforts in collecting funds from others. Besides, he gave his time and personal attention to the erection of the building, and when it was complete he, his father, William G. Jones, and Jacob M. Chalfant, gave their individual notes for ten thousand dollars debt remaining upon it. Mr. Jones was then, and has been ever since, the largest contributor to the funds of this church. It is remarkable that while engrossed in building a new house of worship they contributed more to Christian benevolence abroad than in former years, and enjoyed besides a gracious revival and large accessions.

On the 3d of May, 1855, the new and handsome house of worship was dedicated. The sermon was preached by Rev. Benj. Griffith, D. D. The twenty-fifth anniversary of the opening was commemorated May, 1880. In preparation for this, nearly one thousand dollars were raised and expended for painting and repairs; and as much more being required for the same purpose, Mr. S. A. Hodgman proposed that three thousand dollars be raised—two thousand dollars to pay off the debt of the church contracted for improvements some years ago. On Sunday morning, February 22, 1880, Mr. Washington Jones secured the whole amount, and the house, handsomely frescoed, was reopened May 16 and 17, 1880, with appropriate exercises. The Committee having the work in charge—Alfred Gawthrop, George A. Le Maistre, and Edgar H. Quinby—did their work well.

The present membership is three hundred and sixty-six, with two Sunday-schools and six hundred and sixty-seven scholars and teachers. This church has enjoyed in its history, extending over nearly fifty years, five great revivals. In 1842, under Rev. Sandford Leach, aided by Rev. Emerson Andrews, evangelist, the membership was increased from seventy-nine to two hundred. In 1843–44, under Rev. M. J. Rhees, D. D., assisted by Elder Jacob Knapp, one hundred and fifty-six were converted. In 1854, under Rev. Frederick Charlton, their number advanced from three hundred and fifteen to four hundred and one. In 1865, under Rev.

J. S. Dickerson, D. D., assisted by Elder Jacob Knapp, one hundred and ninety-four were added. In 1876, during the present pastorate, one hundred and seventy-two united with the church. In 1867, the Philadelphia Association met with this church.

The following is a list of Pastors, with the dates of their service: Rev. Jonathan G. Collom first served the church as supply for three months. Rev. C. W. Dennison, from September 9, 1836, to February 25, 1839. Rev. George Carleton, from September 15, 1839, to April 14, 1841. Rev. Sandford Leach, from July 1, 1841, to June 17, 1842. Rev. Morgan J. Rhees, D. D., from April 2, 1843, to May 27, 1850. Rev. Jonathan G. Collom, from August 1, 1850, to March 22, 1853. Rev. Frederick Charlton, from June 27, 1853, to August, 1857. Rev. George M. Condron, from April 1, 1858 to October 1, 1859. Rev. James S. Dickerson, D. D., from March 1, 1861, to May, 1865. Rev. W. H. H. Marsh, from September 1, 1865, to March 26, 1871. Rev. James Waters, from March 24, 1872, to November 16, 1873. Rev. Alexander McArthur, from March, 1874, to September, 1875. Rev.

Richard B. Cook, the present Pastor, who came December 1, 1875.

Prior to the formation of this church a few members—sixteen in number—withdrew from the First Church, and formed themselves into a church which appears on the Minutes of the Delaware Association as the Second of Wilmington. It was organized April 4, 1814, and received into the Association the same year, William G. Jones being one of the messengers to receive the hand of fellowship. But this church was dissolved February 5, 1816. Mr. Jones did not go back to the First Church, but united with that at Marcus Hook. He was very active in the present Second Church, however, from the start, though he did not become a member there until the pastorate of Mr. Leach, who, when called by the church, made this the condition of his acceptance — that Mr. Jones bring his letter. It was done, and Mr. Jones from that time till his death was Deacon of the church. His house was the "Baptist Hotel" throughout his time, and many of the leading men of his day enjoyed his hospitality.

REV. R. B. COOK.

P. 102.

2. Dover Church, 1852.

The second existing church formed in the State was that at Dover in 1852. In 1832, George Parris came to the neighborhood of Dover from New Jersey. No Baptists of our faith and order were there then except Jonathan Stites and Mary his wife, also from New Jersey, who preceded Mr. Parris about two years. They were intelligent Christians, and adorned by their walk and talk the Christian life for many years, both dying in 1869. Rev. John P. Thompson, an old man, and formerly a sailor, came to Dover and vicinity, and labored for several years for a small salary from the American Baptist Home Mission Society and for what could be collected on the field. He and others labored up to August, 1847, when Rev. John P. Walter was persuaded to come to Dover. He came October 1st as missionary on a salary of three hundred dollars, of which amount one hundred dollars were provided by the American Baptist Home Mission Society, one hundred dollars by the Second Church, Wilmington, and one hundred dollars were assumed by Mr. Parris to be collected on the field.

In 1850, a subscription was started for a house of worship; Brethren Stites and Parris gave five hundred dollars each toward it. Besides, they had bought the parsonage and ground next to it, facing the Public Square, whereon the church now stands, in 1848 and 1849, in trust for the Baptist Church, which was not incorporated till 1853. The corner-stone of the new house was laid, September 9, 1850, by Rev. A. D. Gillette, D. D., of Philadelphia, and the basement dedicated, January 25, 1852, at which time the church was constituted with eight members—Jonathan Stites, Mary Stites, George Parris, Jane E. Parris his wife, George P. Barker and Ruth Barker his wife, Elizabeth Walker, and Beulah Magonagill. The two latter were daughters of Stites and wife. Mrs. Walker was the only one living in Dover, the others living in the country. Rev. J. G. Collom, Pastor of the Second Church, Wilmington, officiated at the constitution of the church. Mr. Walter became Pastor of the church, and worked with his own hands to get the house built. He resigned July 1, 1852, and was succeeded by Rev. D. A. Nichols, who resigned in 1853. Rev. E. R. Hera succeeded

REV. O. F. FLIPPO. P. 105.

Mr. Nichols, and left in 1854. From 1854 to 1859 the church had no Pastor. Rev. C. J. Hopkins became Pastor in 1859, but retained his charge only three months. The church was without a Pastor until 1861, when Rev. H. C. Putnam settled with them. He resigned September 20, 1863. They were again without a Pastor until 1866, when Rev. D. B. Purinton was sent to Dover by the American Baptist Home Mission Society. He resigned the charge of the Dover Church in 1868, and was succeeded by Rev. O. F. Flippo in March of the same year, who remained Pastor for over two years. While Pastor he baptized nearly one hundred believers. Before this there had not been a baptism nor an accession for nearly two years. The church-doors even had been closed, and all was cheerless and discouraging. November 8, 1869, Mr. Flippo left for a time to collect funds for the purchase of the Wyoming Institute for the Baptist denomination. Rev. George Bradford supplied the pulpit during his absence. Mr. Flippo resigned, September 15, 1870, to become General Missionary of the American Baptist Home Mission Society in Delaware and to give attention to the Wyoming Institute.

The coming of Mr. Flippo into the State was followed by an awakening among our churches and a growth of Baptist sentiment. We are reminded of the labors of Messrs. Baker and Hughes nearly a hundred years before. He was instrumental in the formation of several new churches, one of which came over to the Baptists from another denomination, Pastor and all. He was also the means of purchasing for the denomination, at a reasonable price, the Wyoming Institute, and was its first President. He also edited and published in the State *The Baptist Visitor*, by which our history, work, and principles were brought before the people, and much good done. The frequent invitations he received and accepted to present our views in sermons or lectures was another means of extending our principles and multiplying our churches. "It pays," he wrote, "to cultivate Delaware." In all his work, Mr. Flippo was aided by Rev. George Bradford, Rev. N. C. Naylor, and Rev. Dr. Isaac Cole, who rendered him efficient service. Mr. Flippo felt that he had hardly begun his work in Delaware when it became apparent that he must seek a change of climate for his wife, and a field of labor

REV. JEREMIAH GRIMMEL. P. 107.

where he could be more at home during her decline. In March, 1873, he left the State to accept a pastorate in Maryland, and a few months afterward his wife died. The Dover Church had no Pastor from 1870 to 1873. Rev. Charles Harrison was Pastor from February 27 to September 27, 1873. There was no Pastor from 1873 to 1875. Rev. J. J. Reader was called April 18, 1875, and resigned October 1, 1876. Rev. B. G. Parker, the present Pastor, was called October 29, 1876.

3. First German Church, Wilmington, 1856.

Rev. J. M. Hoefflin says: "In the year 1855, a German Baptist, Jeremiah Grimmell by name, a bookbinder by trade, came to Wilmington, Delaware. He was a native of Marburg in Hessen, where he was banished from house and home on account of his free confession of Jesus Christ, the only Saviour of the lost world." The Rev. Julius C. Grimmell, Pastor of the German Baptist Church, Brooklyn, New York, and son of Jeremiah Grimmell, writes: "Father was born January 25, 1809, converted in 1835, and baptized October 25th of the same

year, at midnight, in the river Lahn, by J. G. Oncken of Hamburg. He endured bitter persecution, the loss of property and business, and was often held in prison up to the year 1848. In 1851, he came to America, where he first gained converts in Williamsburg, thus laying the foundation of the church over which I am Pastor. . . . In 1867, he made Buffalo, N. Y., his home, helping his son, then Pastor of the First German Baptist Church, as a most desirable aid and adviser. He died while on a visit to his beloved Wilmington, April 4, 1871."
"In accordance with his own conviction," continues Mr. Hoefflin, "Mr. Grimmell, now being in the land of gospel liberty, improved his opportunity to bring the joyful tidings of salvation through faith in the Lord Jesus Christ to his German friends, making, in this way a faithful use of his spare hours, and making even more spare hours for this very purpose than the wants of his family well permitted of; but the love of Christ constrained him thus to devote much of his time to making known the precious news which had gladdened his heart and brightened his path. Miss Anne Semple found him once in an upper room, his shop,

working industriously, and all the while talking to a young woman, an inquirer, whose tears were freely flowing. After some personal contact in visiting with his German friends, he invited them to a religious meeting in his dwelling-house, where a number met with him. The number thus meeting together increased rapidly, so that his own room was found too small; when a neighbor, Mr. John Schwager, who afterward proved one of the first converts, kindly opened his basement, on the corner of Pine and Fourth Streets, where the meetings were held for a long while. After some time the brethren of the Second Baptist Church gave them the use of their lecture-room, on the corner of Fifth and Walnut Streets, where their meetings were held for some time, until the church was rented; then they received short notice to vacate the place, and were obliged to return into the basement of Mr. J. Schwager's house.

"Meanwhile, Rev. Conrad Fleischmann, Pastor of the First German Church in Philadelphia, had come down to Wilmington several times to proclaim the word of life to the gathered company. The Lord signally blessed the labors of both Mr. J. Grimmell and Rev. C. Fleischmann, so that at the end of nine months there were seven persons hopefully converted, who were baptized on the second day of March, 1856, by Mr. Fleischmann. Two weeks later, five others professed Christ precious to their souls, and were also baptized by Mr. Fleischmann. The baptisms took place in the Second Baptist Church, corner Fourth and French Streets. In consequence of this most glorious beginning the Lord touched the heart of a member then of the Second Baptist Church—Miss Anne Semple—to assist this young band of German Baptists to obtain a house of worship for them, equal to their pressing demand. Miss Semple effected the purchase of the old church, corner Fifth and Walnut Streets, for three thousand dollars, of which sum she donated a large share. Prior to the purchase they worshipped in her parlor.

"After the purchase of the building it was deemed necessary to organize a church. The organization was effected on the 17th of April, 1856. The following were the original constituents of the First German Baptist Church: Jeremiah Grimmell and wife Margaret, Edward Austermühl, John Mühlhausen and wife Sophia, John Schwager and wife Elizabeth, Peter Braunstein and wife Susan, Frederick Neutze, Mrs. Elizabeth Kaiser, Mrs. Theresa Hirzel, Catherine Braunstein. Of the above there are still eight in number spared to the church to the present day. The church had rather a slow growth, but at the same time a healthful one. The total number of those that united with the church during the entire history is one hundred and sixty-four. The present membership is seventy-seven. The church-property is free from debt.

"Since the organization there have been six Pastors laboring with the church, the present one included. In the month of December, 1856, the church called the first Pastor, Rev. F. A. Bauer, who remained with the church about one year and a half. Their second Pastor was Rev. J. C. Haselhuhn, now editor of the religious periodical of the German Baptists of North America, called *Der Sendbote*, who remained with the church a little over three years. Rev. H. Trumpp became their third Pastor, who remained with them a little over four years. Rev. R. Piepgrass was their fourth

Pastor, and remained with them but one year. Rev. J. Fellman became their fifth Pastor, and remained with them about five years. The sixth one is their present Pastor, Rev. J. M. Hoefflin, who settled with them, November 1, 1875."

4. Delaware Avenue Church, Wilmington, 1865.

"A sister of the Second Baptist Church, from no other motive than to advance the cause of Christ and the interest of the denomination, and knowing the need of another church in a growing part of the city, induced fifteen members to unite and form a new interest remote from the Second Church, under the name of the Delaware Avenue Baptist Church."

They were dismissed for the purpose from the Second Church, and constituted a church in May, 1865. Their names were as follows: Anne Semple, Alexander Bratton, Mary Slack, Mary A. Bratton, Kate Bratton, Amanda Bratton, Marion Moore, Mary Smith, Thomas C. Kees, W. H. Gregg, Lucy V. Gregg, John Bradford, Rebecca Bradford, Eliza Jane Cloward, Charles Townsend. The organization

DELAWARE AVENUE BAPTIST CHURCH.

P. 112.

was effected in the house of Miss Anne Semple, June 22, when and where Anne Semple, Mary Slack, and W. H. Gregg were appointed a Committee to prepare Articles of Faith and a Church Covenant. The Committee recommended the *Baptist Church Manual*, which was adopted. These three members became the largest contributors to the current expenses and building fund of the church, the contributions of Miss Slack amounting in the aggregate to ten thousand dollars. The church was recognized as a regular Baptist Church by a Council convened in the Second Church, July 6, 1865, and received into the Philadelphia Association the same year.

After their organization the new church worshipped for some time in the Wilmington Institute (Scientific Lecture-room), and held its week-night meetings in the Phœnix Enginehouse, the latter free of charge. In October, 1865, however, they leased the meeting-house of the old First Church. The sister before named as originator of this movement presented the church with a lot, which was exchanged for the one on the corner of Delaware Avenue and West Street, upon which their large brownstone house of worship stands in one of the best locations.

Rev. George W. Folwell became their Pastor April 1, 1866. Their number then was fifty. The lecture-room of the new house was dedicated January 2, 1868, and the audience-room, October 13, 1870. The total value of their church-property is estimated at sixty-five thousand dollars. They are still, however, greatly in debt, despite their heroic struggles and self-sacrifices; but the day is not far distant, they hope, when all encumbrances will be removed. A corner lot, eighty by one hundred feet, was given them by Mr. Philip McDowel at McDowelville, on the outskirts of the city, upon which they have recently built and dedicated a chapel, and in which they maintain a mission-school.

Mr. Folwell resigned October 1, 1874, the church numbering when he left them two hundred and forty-six. He was succeeded by the present Pastor, Rev. Isaac M. Haldeman, April 11, 1875. In the interval the pulpit was supplied by Rev. T. A. Gill, U. S. N. Under Mr. Haldeman's ministrations the membership has been increased to about one thousand. Three

REV. D. B. PURINTON.

hundred and seventy-six baptisms were reported in 1876, and one hundred and three in 1878 Mr. S. R. Ball informs the writer that the seating capacity of the meeting-house has been increased to twelve hundred, and that it is almost always full.

5. Plymouth Church, 1867–73.

In December, 1866, Rev. D. B. Purinton came to Dover under the auspices of the American Baptist Home Mission Society. He found several Baptist families residing in Plymouth, ten miles south of Dover. In February, 1867, he began preaching on Tuesday evenings once in two weeks, until the following April, when he commenced services on Lord's Day afternoon of every other week—in the Congregational house of worship generally, but sometimes in private houses. Several more Baptist families having moved into the vicinity during the spring, a church was formed May 29, 1867, recognized September 24, 1867, and admitted into the Philadelphia Association, October 2 of the same year. Thirty members constituted the church, all of them from the Northern or Eastern States. Among them were Rev. E. P.

Salisbury and family, and Deacon F. C. Mack and his family.

Mr. Purinton preached for them till March, 1868, when he removed to New York State, but, returning in May, became Pastor of the church in June, preaching for them on Lord's Day, and during the week laboring in Lower Delaware and Maryland. He resigned, however, in February, 1871, to take pastoral charge of a church in New York. He finally returned to Delaware, where he died in 1876. Deacon Mack writes of him: "To the blessing of God upon his labors is due the re-establishment of Baptist churches in this part of Delaware. He labored, and other men entered upon his labors." He was a brother-in-law of Rev. A. B. Earle, D. D., the evangelist.

Rev. J. M. Haswell, the missionary, while residing in the State preached for them occasionally, as did also Rev. Dr. Isaac Cole, but sometimes, when they had no preaching, one of the members read a sermon, generally from the *Examiner*, to those assembled. The church being weakened by a number of the members returning to their former homes, and being unable, with no house, to have regular times of worship, disbanded March 22, 1873, to unite with others in forming the church at Magnolia.*

For most of the above facts I am indebted to Mr. E. H. Salisbury, son of Rev. E. P. Salisbury, who, with his widowed mother, resides in the State.

6. Lincoln Church, 1869–73.

A meeting was held in May, 1867, at Lincoln, near Milford, in the house of Mr. A M. Webb, to organize a Baptist Church. Sixteen persons out of twenty-three Baptists residing within eight miles of the place were present. Rev. W. H. Spencer and Rev. W. H. H. Dwyer, as well as Mr. Webb, greatly favored the enterprise, but the project failed. Shortly afterward Miss E. C. Parham came into the neighborhood from Milestown, Pennsylvania, and, being a strong Baptist, gave new hope to the cause. With the assistance of Rev. D. B. Purinton a church was finally organized, April

* The reference to the union of the Plymouth and Lincoln churches with those of Milford and Magnolia respectively, found in a note on p. 13 of Philadelphia Association Minutes, 1873, is just the reverse of what was the case.

28, 1869, with twenty-one members. W. C. Coles was elected Deacon, and A. M. Webb, Clerk. Rev. Messrs. Flippo and Purinton preached for them at times. A Council, composed of Rev. Messrs. Marsh, Folwell, Flippo, Purinton, and Hope, and other messengers of the churches, was organized, with Rev. D. B. Purinton as Moderator and Alfred Gawthrop as Clerk, and recognized them as a church. Rev. W. H. Spencer became Pastor, and upon his death A. M. Webb was licensed to preach, and continued to fill the pulpit until the church disbanded to unite with others in the formation of the Milford Church in 1873.

7. Zion Church, 1871.

While engaged in his work of General Missionary, Mr. Flippo was invited to preach at Vernon, Kent County, where was a congregation of Independent Methodists (Methodist Protestants). He first complied with their request December, 1870. They soon sent for him again, and invited him to hold a protracted meeting, which he did, preaching to sinners every night. This was in the spring of 1871. In the midst of the meeting they approached him with the request to preach a series of sermons on the Principles and Practices of Baptists. They were inquiring, and wanted to know who we were and where we came from. He agreed to do so, on condition that they would follow him through "with the New Testament in hand, and not get mad." This they consented to do. He commenced a series of lectures upon the doctrines we hold. Before he was through with the lectures every member, Pastor and all, was ready to be baptized, and applied for baptism; and the whole church was baptized. Rev. Richard H. Merriken, since called to his reward, was then Pastor. The baptism occurred on a stormy day, March 12, 1871.

On the last Lord's Day in April, 1871, the church was organized and recognized, Rev. J. M. Hope, Rev. W. H. Spencer, and Rev. O. F. Flippo officiating. On the same day Rev. R. H. Merriken was ordained to the work of the Baptist ministry. The little band started a subscription for a new house of worship, and in November of the same year dedicated, nearly free of debt, a beautiful Gothic chapel. Mr. Flippo preached the dedicatory sermon. This church is called the Zion Baptist Church. They have received large accessions since, and have always been faithful to the truth. The members of this church, for the most part, devote one-tenth of all their products annually to the Lord. They have a flourishing Sunday-school, under the superintendence of W. W. Seeders.

Rev. M. Heath and Rev. J. M. Hope were co-Pastors of this church for some time. The present Pastor is Rev. George Bradford, who is a native of Virginia, and came into the State in 1869 to supply the Dover Church. Since that time he has devoted himself mainly to self-denying labor in needy Delaware. Mr. Bradford mentions Deacon Andrew Burnham, formerly of Vermont, as one to whose efforts in a great measure, and in connection with Mr. Flippo, the church owes its existence.

8. Wyoming Church, 1872.

The Wyoming Church was organized in 1872. While Pastor at Dover, Mr. Flippo was invited to preach in the chapel of the Institute at Wyoming. A revival broke out in the school, and a number were converted. Sev-

REV. JAMES M. HOPE.

eral persons living in Wyoming were baptized, and united with the Dover Baptist Church, and others were hesitating at the water, and efforts were about to be made to build a meetinghouse. It was then that the Trustees approached with the offer to sell the Institute. It was purchased, and in April, 1872, the church was formed, letters being granted by the Dover Church for that purpose. Rev. James Waters, Rev. G. W. Folwell, Rev. A. F. Shanafelt, Rev. E. E. Maryatt, Rev. J. M. Hope, and Rev. O. F. Flippo were present. The chapel in the Institute building was dedicated as a house of worship, Rev. J. S. Backus, D. D., of New York, preaching the sermon. Rev. M. Heath and Rev. J. M. Hope were co-Pastors of this, in connection with the Zion Church. Rev. George Bradford now serves as Pastor for both of these churches. He is assisted by Messrs. Miles S. Read, William S. Read, and other students from Crozer Theological Seminary, Chester, Pennsylvania.

9. Magnolia Church, 1873.

In March, 1872, Mr. Flippo was invited to preach in the village of Magnolia. He introduced Baptist principles in the first sermon in love and kindness. They heard the word gladly, and from time to time believers were baptized. The Plymouth Church had been formed in 1867, but, having no house of worship, disbanded, and united with the baptized believers at Magnolia in the organization of the Magnolia Church. On the 3d of April the church was recognized, and the corner-stone of a new chapel was laid by Mr. Flippo. Rev. M. Heath was the first Pastor of this church, in which relation he continued for two years. Rev. J. M. Hope preached alternately with him, and is now sole Pastor of the church.

10. Milford Church, 1873.

A church was organized at Milford, with nineteen members, June 14, 1873. Some of these were from the disbanded Lincoln Church. The church was organized in the old Methodist meeting-house, and was formed mainly through the efforts of Rev. Messrs. J. M. Hope, Shaffer, and A. M. Webb. The house of worship at Milford was dedicated on Thanksgiving Day, 1875. Rev. Thomas Swaim, D. D., preached in the morning, and Rev. J. M. Hope at night.

Money enough was then raised to leave but a small indebtedness on the house, which is a substantial one and in a good location.

11. Elm Street, 1873–76.

July 30, 1873, was organized the Elm Street Church, Wilmington. Rev. N. C. Naylor, who had labored with them when a mission, became their Pastor. This interest grew out of the Baptist City Mission. The only other Pastor this church had was Rev. R. E. Bartlett, who was called to the ministry and ordained there. This church disbanded December, 1876.

12. Shiloh Church, 1876.

The first African Baptist Church in Delaware was formed in Wilmington in the Centennial year (1876), under the name of Shiloh, with twenty-one members. This church originated from a Sunday-school started in the interest of the colored people by members of the First Church, after its return to the Philadelphia Association, and during the pastorate of Rev. Thomas M. Eastwood. Most of the constituent members were either baptized by him, or received by letter or experience into the First

Church, with the understanding that as soon as a sufficient number could be brought together a colored Baptist Church should be formed. They worship in a rented hall, but have a lot in a good location, on which they hope soon to build. They have a membership of eighty, and a congregation filling the room in which they meet, and greatly need a house of their own. Rev. B. T. Moore, a graduate of the Wayland Seminary, Washington, D. C., is Pastor; they have had no other.

13. New Castle Church, 1876.

In the same year (1876) the New Castle Church, composed of fourteen members, was received into the fellowship of Baptist churches. It was constituted September 30, recognized February 13, 1877, and received into the Philadelphia Association in October, 1877. It originated through the labors of Rev. B. MacMackin and Rev. William H. Young, then students at Crozer Theological Seminary. It was during the Senior year that the needs of Delaware pressed upon the former. Failing to start others in the work, he and Mr. Young agreed to do what they could themselves. In 1875, they

NEWCASTLE BAPTIST CHURCH.

P. 124.

decided to begin work at New Castle, as the place most accessible and needy. They knew nobody there, nor did they think there were any Baptists in the town. They resolved to establish a Bible school, but the court-house was the only place suitable. The chief-justice positively refused its use for religious services, but finally it was secured without his knowledge. Then friends were raised up for them, and Sunday afternoon, January 17, 1876, the Bible school was started, and soon there were two hundred adults collected regularly for the study of God's word. The school-service was followed by a sermon; some Baptists, previously unknown to each other as such, were collected; several others were converted and baptized; and a Baptist Church was constituted September 30, 1876, composed of fourteen members.

The work was supported entirely by the private means of these two brethren, excepting twenty-five dollars given toward an organ by three friends, what was taken up in collections, and a present of twenty-five Bibles from Mrs. John P. Crozer. "They found, however, a lady—Mrs. Jonathan George, living just outside the town—who was noted for her loyalty to our denomination and her tireless energy in all she did. For years she had been trying to urge some one to begin work in New Castle, and thus she gladly joined with these brethren in a way that was as effectual as it was gratifying. In fact, the interest at New Castle owes its existence greatly to the timely assistance of this earnest lady."

"In 1877, Mr. MacMackin became Pastor of the church. In April, 1878, the corner-stone of their church-building was laid. Since then," continues Mr. Young, "Brother MacMackin has been doing yeoman service in building the church-edifice," and "has been Pastor and preacher of the church, as well as architect, contractor, builder, and financial agent of the edifice." The house, a beautiful Gothic of extra fine brick, capable of seating three hundred persons, with slate roof, five stained windows, and neat belfry, costing, with the lot, over six thousand dollars, was dedicated, free of debt, December 19, 1879. The membership is now sixty-four. Among the noble contributors to the building fund, living out of the State and mentioned by Mr. Mac-

Mackin, are Messrs. W. E. Garrett, Benjamin Gartside, Sr., Samuel A. Crozer, Callaghan Bros., J. J. Stadiger, and Mrs. J. P. Crozer.

14. BETHANY CHURCH, 1878.

July 2, 1868, a motion was passed at a regular meeting of "The Baptist Church" of Wilmington (the old First) to receive members by letter from other Baptist churches. A similar motion had been passed some years before, and rescinded by them. At this meeting—in 1868—and immediately after the passage of the resolution, there were received, from Delaware Avenue Church, William H. Gregg, Lucy V. Gregg, and John Galbraith. Messrs. Gregg and Galbraith were appointed a Committee to secure from the Presbyterians, who had leased the house on King Street, the use of it for Sunday-school and prayer-meeting purposes. Being refused, a Sunday-school was started in the second story of the Friendship Engine-house, which at the end of the year—the lease of the Presbyterians having expired—was removed to the church, and met with large success. A prayer-meeting was also held, and as there were now constant accessions by letter, new life and activity were infused. In October, 1871, the church made application to the Philadelphia Association to be reinstated in that body, and was received and restored to its former place on the roll, with the date 1785 as that of its organization.

On April 13, 1871, Rev. E. E. Maryatt, a graduate of Crozer Theological Seminary, was chosen Pastor. He entered upon his work September 1st, and was ordained on the 28th of the same month. He served the church until August 22, 1873, when he resigned, and left with the high regard of all. Regular services were then conducted by students from Crozer Seminary and others. On April 21, 1874, Rev. Thomas M. Eastwood was elected Pastor, and ordained June 11th of the same year. He was a native of Pennsylvania, who graduated at the University at Lewisburg, and afterward studied at the Crozer Theological Seminary. He began to minister statedly to the church, May 1, 1874.

In December, 1876, the First Church emigrated from its old field to that which had been occupied by the Elm Street Baptist Church, in the south-western part of the city. The Elm

REV. THOMAS M. EASTWOOD.

Street Church disbanded because unable to maintain itself, and united with the First Church, which came to cultivate this important field and occupy the house. The chapel and lot, however, belonged to the Baptist City Mission, composed of all the Baptist churches of the city. At a regular meeting of the "Mission," held October 14, 1878, it was voted to present "to the brethren now worshipping in Elm Street Chapel, under whatever name they may hereafter assume," the entire property owned by it at the corner of Elm and Jackson Streets. After being in Elm Street Chapel for about two years, it was decided to disband the organization known as the First Baptist Church, and to reorganize under another name. The church disbanded, and the Bethany Baptist Church was formed, November 7, 1878, with Rev. Thomas M. Eastwood as Pastor, and was recognized by a Council, January 2, 1879. At present the church is in a growing condition, with a membership of one hundred and ten and a Sunday-school of two hundred and seventy scholars.

15. THE WILMINGTON BAPTIST CITY MISSION, 1870.

The "City Mission" referred to was organized, upon the Newark (N. J.) plan, in 1870, February 21st, in the Delaware Avenue Church. Washington Jones was chosen President; Frank Braunstein, Vice-President; Maury James, Secretary; and William H. Gregg, Treasurer. The "Mission" is composed of the Pastors and delegates of the Wilmington Baptist churches. It succeeded in buying a large and eligible lot on the corner of Elm and Jackson Streets for eighteen hundred dollars, of which eight hundred were paid, and the remainder left upon mortgage. A chapel costing three thousand two hundred and fifty dollars was soon after erected, and finally paid for. This property was used by the Elm Street Church until the organization of the Bethany Church, when it was deeded to the latter.

16. THE WYOMING INSTITUTE, 1869.

In 1869, the Baptists purchased, through the agency of Rev. O. F. Flippo, the Wyoming Institute, at Wyoming, three miles south of

Dover. The building was furnished for a school of over one hundred, accommodated with a chapel, and surrounded by four acres of ground. A new and liberal charter was obtained in 1875, since which time the Institute has had its annual graduating classes. It is for both sexes. There are two departments—the Preparatory, for common branches, and the Seminary course of three years, for graduation. For several years past it has enjoyed a high degree of prosperity, at times reaching the utmost limits of its accommodations.

The Principal, Rev. M. Heath, A. M., who has held the position the past seven years, is a native of New Jersey and a graduate of Madison University, New York. For the past fifteen years he has been successfully connected with educational interests. It is with gratification we hear of the success of this institution, and trust that the Baptists of Delaware will show their appreciation of the privilege it affords, and support it by their prayers, their means, and by sending their sons and daughters to Wyoming to be educated.

17. The Delaware Baptist Union, 1878.

The *Baptist Visitor* having advocated, especially in September, 1869, the consolidation of the Baptists in the State, a Committee met in the Baptist Church, Dover, November 3, 1870, which resulted in the drafting of a Constitution and By-Laws for a Delaware Association. This Committee consisted of Rev. W. H. H. Marsh, E. W. Dickinson, D. D., Rev. G. W. Folwell, Rev. O. F. Flippo, and R. W. L. Probasco. They failed to get their Association, for "love for the old Philadelphia was too strong," but eventually the "Delaware Baptist Missionary Union" was formed at Wyoming, June 25, 1874. A large meeting at Dover in September of the same year confirmed the action. This body met annually in September, but quarterly meetings were provided for, to be conducted by committees appointed at the annual meeting.

The object of this organization was "to cultivate the destitute field, and to encourage the feeble churches within its bounds." It was felt, however, that something more was needed, and brethren talked again of forming an Association for Delaware. But separation and change of name would hardly supply the lack of numbers and strength.

In pursuance of a call signed by ministers in Delaware and Pennsylvania, a Council convened in the First Baptist Church, Chester, Pennsylvania, November 20, 1876, to "*consider*" "the expediency" of forming a "South Philadelphia Association," to be composed of such of the Baptist churches of Delaware State, Delaware County, Pennsylvania, and Philadelphia as favored the movement. The Council met, and was well attended. Rev. J. Wheaton Smith, D. D., was chosen Moderator, and Rev. R. B. Cook, Clerk.

This Council has been regarded as a failure by some, but it did not fail to *consider* the subject before it; and more, it demonstrated several things: That Philadelphia churches were not as ready to break from their present connections as some thought; that union of Delaware County and Delaware State churches with those of Philadelphia in a new Association was neither possible nor desirable; that no union, even among the churches of Delaware County and State, could be effected upon the basis of separation from the Philadelphia Association.

Moreover, the Council appointed a Committee, consisting of Rev. R. B. Cook, H. G. Weston, D. D., J. Wheaton Smith, D. D., Rev. P. L. Jones, and Rev. Z. T. Dowen, to work up the matter and to call another Council at the proper time and place. There were members of the Committee and others who were not idle in the matter. The protracted illness of the Chairman caused delay, but finally a meeting of the then existing "Delaware Baptist Missionary Union" was arranged for, by Brethren Eastwood, MacMackin, Parker, and the Chairman of the Committee, to meet at Dover in May, 1878.

The meeting was largely attended by the brethren from Wilmington. It was agreed upon to reorganize and enlarge at the next meeting, and to invite the churches of Delaware County, Pennsylvania, and the Faculty of Crozer Theological Seminary to meet with them and unite in forming the new organization. The meeting was called, and held September 30 and October 1, 1878, in the Second Baptist Church, Wilmington. President H. G. Weston, D. D., preached the opening sermon. Rev. Thomas M. Eastwood was chosen

HENRY G. WESTON, D.D.

Moderator, and Rev. B. G. Parker, Clerk, both *pro tem*. A Committee, consisting of Rev. R. B. Cook, Rev. A. G. Thomas, Rev. Alexander McArthur, Rev. H. B. Harper, Rev. J. R. Downer, and G. D. B. Pepper, D. D., was appointed to prepare a plan of organization. The formation of a Union was recommended, and a plan of organization proposed. The report was adopted, and the "Delaware Baptist Union" was organized October 1, 1878.

The "Union" was to be composed of such churches of Delaware State, Delaware County, Pennsylvania, and vicinity as were then present by delegates or Pastor, and such as should afterward be admitted, upon application, by a two-thirds vote. Each church is entitled to appoint five delegates, including the Pastor; and the time of meeting, the third Tuesday and Wednesday in November and the second Tuesday and Wednesday in May. In November, is the Annual Meeting, at which officers are elected for the year.

The object of the "Union" is the promotion of fraternity among the churches united, and the evangelization of the field. It is required that ample time be given, at each meeting, for verbal reports from the churches and for the consideration of Home and Foreign Missions, Education, Bible, Publication, and Sunday-school work. Committees are provided for on — Place of Meeting; Religious Exercises; Pastoral Interchange in Revival Work; The Spiritual Condition of the Field—its want and supply; and Sunday-schools. The two latter were added at a subsequent meeting.

Upon the organization of the Union, Rev. T. M. Eastwood was elected Moderator, Rev. B. G. Parker, Clerk, and Deacon George Parris, Treasurer. A meeting was appointed for an early day at Chester, Pennsylvania, where the Union met with the First Church, Rev. A. G. Thomas, Pastor, November 19 and 20, 1878. Another was held with the church at Milford, Delaware, May 13 and 14, 1879, which proved a most successful meeting for members, and interest and effect upon the community and church. There were sixty delegates present, who were warmly welcomed by the Pastor, Rev. W. H. Young, by the church, and by the people at large. The November meeting for 1879 was held with the church at Media, Pennsylvania, Rev. T. G. Wright, Pastor, where the Union also met with a cordial reception. The meeting in May, 1880, was at Dover, Delaware, and was largely attended, as well as profitable and pleasant.

Through the efforts of the "Union," pastors and students have gone to various points to labor, and their expenses have been paid; and a Colporteur and Sunday-school Missionary, Rev. Wm. H. Young, appointed by the Baptist Publication Society to labor in Delaware. Mr. Young has resigned on account of ill-health, and it is to be hoped that his successor will soon be named.

Some of the prominent laymen connected with the Union are—James Irving, William H. Gregg, Washington Jones, Benj. Gartside, Sr., Dr. J. B. Weston, George Parris, P. Miles Frame, F. C. Mack, G. E. Heyburn, William Russell, J. M. Tage, A. B. Stewart, E. Ainsworth, Deacon Duffee, J. H. George, Elnathan Smith, E. H. Salisbury, Absalom H. Carey, Harry Emmons, G. P. Barker, and Dr. Frederic Owens. And among those, besides the pastors of the churches, who have already participated by sermon, paper, or address in the meetings of this youthful organization, and thus helped make them pleasant and profitable are—President H. G. Weston, D. D., William Cathcart, D. D., Prof. G. R. Bliss, D. D., J. M. Pendleton, D. D., Prof. J. C. Long, D. D., Rev. G. W. Folwell, Samuel A. Crozer, Esq., Washington Jones, Esq., Alfred Gawthrop, Esq., H. L. Wayland, D. D., Prof. G. D. B. Pepper, D. D., Rev. Alexander McArthur, Rev. Prof. J. R. Downer, Rev. Prof. M. Heath, Rev. P. S. Vreeland, Rev. Dr. S. Dyer, E. F. James, Rev. Owen James, Thomas Swaim, D. D., Rev. David Spencer, and G. J. Johnson, D. D.

The ladies also have had their meetings in behalf of Missions, in connection with those of the "Union." Mrs. Dr. G. D. B. Pepper, Mrs. S. M. Miller, Mrs. George A. LeMaistre, Mrs. P. G. McCollin, Mrs. M. J. Knowlton, and others have by their presence and their addresses contributed very greatly to deepen the interest of Christian women in the work for Missions.

The "Union" consists of eight churches in Pennsylvania and eleven in Delaware, with a total membership in the nineteen churches of about three thousand. The following is a list of the Pastors and churches:

GEO. D. B. PEPPER, D. D.

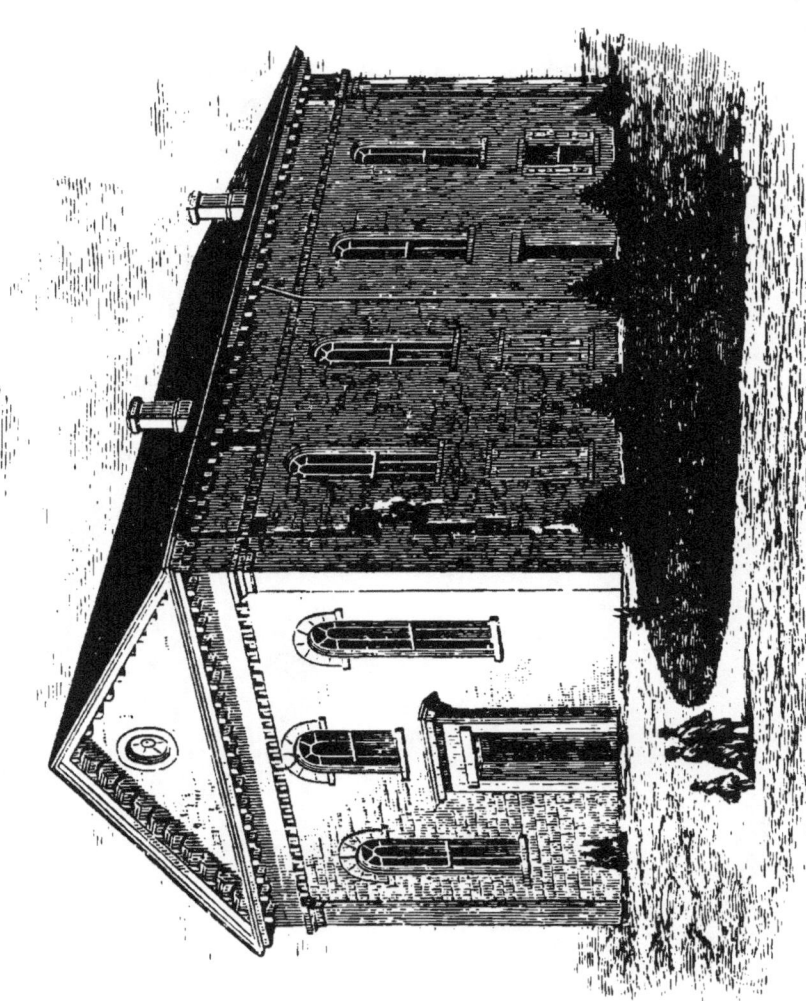

BRANDYWINE CHURCH, DELAWARE COUNTY, PENNA.

IN PENNSYLVANIA.

Brandywine, Rev. J. Wesley Sullivan. Marcus Hook, Rev. C. J. W. Bishop. Ridley, Rev. Charles M. Deitz. First Chester, Rev. A. G. Thomas. South Chester, Rev. H. B. Harper. Media, Rev. T. G. Wright. North Chester, Rev. John Brooks. Village Green, Rev. Miller Jones.

IN DELAWARE.

Second Wilmington, Rev. R. B. Cook. Dover, Rev. B. G. Parker. First German, Wilmington, Rev. J. M. Hoefflin. Delaware Avenue, Rev. J. M. Haldeman. Zion, Vernon, Rev. George Bradford. Wyoming, Rev. George Bradford. Magnolia, Rev. James M. Hope. Milford, Rev. ———. Shiloh, Wilmington, Rev. B. T. Moore. New Castle, Rev. B. MacMackin. Bethany, Wilmington, Rev. T. M. Eastwood.

A list of licentiates and ministers, not Pastors and students for the ministry, connected with the churches of the Union, should not be omitted. The following are the names of those connected with the Union, and not mentioned elsewhere in this work: Ministers—Rev. H. Steelman, Rev. J. S. Read, Rev. Walter Bushell (Missionary), Rev. E. Austermühl; and Licentiates — F. G. McKeever, George Street, Walter Kalley, C. F. Williams, Eugene Maginn, Reuben Blakely, and C. C. Earle.

The present (1880) officers of the Union are —Rev. T. M. Eastwood, Moderator; Rev. H. B. Harper, Clerk; and Deacon George Parris, Treasurer. And the churches belonging to the Delaware Union have not separated from the Philadelphia Association. All the Baptist churches in Delaware, excepting what are known as Old School Baptists, and all within the bounds of the Delaware Union, are connected with the Philadelphia Association.

This part of our subject will be closed with a brief notice of one of our ministers, who was baptized at Wilmington by the Pastor of the First Church of that place. He became a member of that church, and retained his connection with it for some years; and for nearly half a century was the Pastor of two of the churches of the Delaware Baptist Union.

Rev. Joseph Walker was born near Marcus Hook, Delaware County, Pennsylvania, February 14, 1787. He lived with his father upon the farm until his marriage, working indus-

REV. JOSEPH WALKER. P. 140.

triously with his own hands. His conversion took place when he was between eighteen and twenty years of age. His mind seems to have been directed to the subject of religion by a conversation between himself and Mr. William G. Jones, who afterward was his brother-in-law and lifelong friend. Alluding to it in a letter to Mr. Jones, he says: "This was the first personal address I ever had on the subject of religion, except a short talk with my father several years before, when I was on a sick bed." He adds: "After experience and reflection I believe there is nothing so calculated to deeply impress the mind on the subject of religion as personal conversation with a judicious religious friend," and regrets that he had let so many opportunities of this kind pass without improvement. He was baptized by Rev. Daniel Dodge, then Pastor of the First Baptist Church, Wilmington, Delaware, February 6, 1806, at the age of twenty-one. From this time he ever had an humble view of self and an exalted one of Christ. He was ordained to the work of the gospel ministry at Marcus Hook, August 7, 1824, by Rev. William Staughton, D. D., Rev. Daniel Lewis, and Rev. Thomas J. Kitts, and became Pastor of the church, of which he retained the care for twenty years. He had but one other pastorate—the Brandywine Church, Delaware County, Pennsylvania, which he served as Pastor twenty-four years. "In both of these charges he deserved and received the respect and love of all. Mr. Walker was a staunch and thorough-going Baptist; clear and decided in his convictions of Bible truth, unswerving in his loyalty to the Master. In all the relations of life—as a man of business, as a magistrate, as a minister of the gospel—his unimpeachable integrity raised him above malicious criticism. His memory is fragrant in Delaware County, his home for some eighty years." *

Mr. Walker was for more than sixty years a member of the Philadelphia Association; in 1826, he was Clerk; in 1829, Moderator, and for several years President of its Board of Trustees. He was only absent twice in sixty-two years from its regular meetings. The last seven years of his life were spent with his daughter and son-in-law, Dr. Trevor, in Al-

---

* Rev. E. W. Dickinson, D. D.: Obituary Report, Philadelphia Association, 1870.

legheny City, where he died February 28, 1870.

III.—CONCLUSION.

It remains for us to add a few statistics to show the growth and strength of the later Baptist churches in the State of Delaware:

Date.	Churches.	Members.	Contributions.
1835	1	13	No table of contributions published in the Phila. Association Minutes.
1865	4	639	
1875	10	886	$14,190.96
1879	11	1924	20,190.96

The number of teachers and scholars in fourteen Sunday-schools, 2183.

These figures, however, show growth since 1835, which is an evidence of God's favor upon the Missionary Baptists in the State. But more, the later Baptist churches of Delaware belong to a growing people, who have increased in numbers, in the United States alone, from 172,972 in 1812 to 2,133,440 in 1879. Besides their growth at home, their Missions have been successful in foreign lands. In 1814, there were two Missionaries among the heathen, supported by American Baptists, and no Converts. In 1879, belonging to one society alone—The American Baptist Missionary Union—there were 160 Missionaries, 990 Native preachers, 904 Churches, 80,864 Members, all converted heathen, and 18,000 Baptisms during the year. In addition to this, the Bible has been translated into the languages of millions of the human race by the Baptist Missionaries, and by them freely circulated among the heathen and the converts to Christianity. The native Christian converts have their own Conventions, Associations, Schools, and Missions, conducted by themselves. And the total number of baptisms by the Missionaries of the Union up to 1879 is 154,000, or nearly as many as the members of the American Baptist churches when Missions to Asia were inaugurated. We exclaim, "What hath God wrought!" What results from their principles have the Anti-Mission Baptist churches to show, either at home or abroad?

The lesson for us to-day is the necessity of the Missionary spirit to the extension, existence, and perpetuity of the churches of Christ. And these facts regarding both the early and later Baptists should encourage the friends of Jesus, in and out this State, to redouble their efforts to recover lost ground, and to advance the denomination in Delaware to the position of power and influence it would now most probably occupy if there had been no check to its progress in the past. This day, but for the growth of this Anti-Mission evil, the Baptists of this State would be second to none, if not leading in numbers and influence, as they are in some other States. It behooves every Baptist in Delaware to become identified with the work of the denomination in the State, to correspond with the nearest Baptist Pastor, to start a prayer-meeting, or a Sunday-school, or a church in his own dwelling, and call the brethren to help in the work; and, above all, to pray for the prosperity of our Baptist Zion.

The narrow-minded may think that sectarianism prompts this appeal, and that the activity and growth of Baptist churches will be at the cost of other denominations, who would become weaker as we grew stronger. But the reverse of this is true. The Baptists have their part to do in the evangelization of the State; there are sinners to be saved. The prayer is needed here as elsewhere, for more laborers. Faithfulness, and consequent growth, on the part of Baptists would only tend to strengthen the cause of true religion in general, and to make every Christian better and every church stronger.

ADDENDUM.

Since the sketch of the Milford Church (page 122) was stereotyped, it has been ascertained that its Pastors have been Rev. Henry H. Leamy, Rev. Levi Thorne, and Rev. A. S. Bastian.

INDEX.

A.

ACCOMAC JAIL, Rev. E. Baker in, 24.
Adams, Charles Francis, 81.
Adams, John, 80.
Ainger, Abigail, 43.
Ainger, Rachel, 42.
Ainger, Rev. Thomas, 41, 42, 43, 45, 46, 47.
Ainsworth, E., 137.
Almond, William, 47.
American Baptist Home Mission Society, 97, 98, 103, 105, 115.
American Baptist Missionary Union, 82.
American Baptist Publication Society, 69, 71, 87, 137.
Anderson, G., D. D., 66.
Andrews, Rev. Emerson, 100.
Antinomianism, 7, 14, 94, 96.
Arch Street Presbyterian Church, 41.
Austermühl, Rev. Edward, 111, 140.

B.

BACKUS, Rev. J. S., D. D., 121.
Baker, Rev. Elijah, 22–25, 27, 28, 34, 37, 39, 96, 106.
Ball, Mr. S. R., 115.
Bannister, Ann, 97.
Bannister, Moses, 97.
Baptism at midnight in the Lahn, 108.
Baptism in Wilmington by Rev. P. Hughes, 43.
Baptist Church, what it is, 8.
Baptist Church Manual, 113.
Baptist City Mission, Wilmington, 129, 130.
Baptist Education Society, 82.
Baptist General Tract Society, 87.
Baptist Missionary Magazine, 72.
Baptist Tract Magazine, 69, 71.
Baptist Visitor, 106, 132.
Baptists in Pennsylvania, 10.
Barker, George P., 104, 137.
Barker, Ruth, 104.
Bartlett, Rev. R. E., 123.
Barton, Elder Thomas, 22, 87, 91.
Bastian, Rev. A. S., 35, 146.
Batston, Thomas, Esq., 24.
Bauer, Rev. F. A., 111.
Beckley, Robinson, 97.
Benedict, Dr. D., 16, 18, 39, 54, 58, 74, 75.
———, his History of the Baptists, 47, 78, 80, 81.
Benson, Rev. John, 29, 37.

148 INDEX.

Benson, Rev. John, death of, 30.
Beswicks, Vincent, 35.
Bethany Church, Wilmington, 139.
Bethel Church, New Castle County, 38, 64, 76, 77.
Bethel Church, Sussex County, 77.
Bickel, P. W., D. D., 67.
Bishop, Rev. C. J. W., 139.
Blakely, Reuben, 140.
Bliss, Prof. G. R., D. D., 138.
Blockley Church, Philadelphia, 62.
Boggs, Mr. John, Sr., 46.
Boggs, Rev. John, 21, 22, 30, 32, 33, 34, 36, 38, 41, 42, 43, 44.
Boulder, Susanna, 97.
Bradford, Rev. George, 105, 106, 120, 121, 139.
Bradford, John, 112.
Bradford, Rebecca, 112.
Brandywine, Battle of the, 58.
Brandywine Church, 40, 139, 142.
Bratton, Alexander, 112.
Bratton, Amanda, 112.
Bratton, Kate, 112.
Bratton, Mary A., 112.
Braunstein, Catherine, 111.
Braunstein, Frank, 130.
Braunstein, Peter, 111.
Braunstein, Susan, 111.
Broadaway, Rev. Samuel, 36.
Broad Creek Church, 27, 28, 39, 75, 76, 77.
Brooks, Rev. John, 139.
Brown University, 59.
Bryn Zion Church, 31.
Bunyan, John, 36.
Burlington Baptist Church, N. J., 62.
Burnham, Deacon Andrew, 120.
Bush, Mrs. Ann, 40.
Bushell, Rev. Walter, 139.

C.

CALLAGHAN BROTHERS, 127.
Campbell, Mr. William M., 63.
Carey, Absalom H., 137.
Carleton, Rev. George, 101.
Cathcart, William, D. D., 56, 80, 138.
Cathel, Miss Martha, 35.
" Centennial Offering " by Dr. Cathcart, 80.
Central New Jersey Association, 90, 92.
Century Confession, The, 17.
Chalfant, Jacob M., 99.
Charlton, Rev. Frederick, 98, 100, 101.
Chester, First Church, 133, 136, 139.
———, North, Church, 139.
———, South, Church, 139.
Chestnut Hill, first Baptist preaching at, 46.
Church Covenants, introduction of, 17.
Circular Letter first adopted by Philadelphia Association, 53.
Clifton, Daniel, Esq., 35.
Clifton, Mrs. Mary B., 35.
Cloward, Eliza Jane, 112.
Cochran, Jane, 97.
Cohansey Church, N. J., 17.
Cold Spring Baptist Church, 10.
Cole, Rev. Dr. Isaac, 106, 116.
Coles, Deacon W. C., 118.
Coles, Rev. ———, 26.
Collom, Rev. Jonathan G., 101, 104.

INDEX.

Condron, Rev. George M., 101.
Cone, S. H., D. D., 70.
Cook, Rev. R. B., 67, 68, 69, 70, 102, 133, 134, 135, 139.
Cow Marsh Church, 15, 30, 34, 39, 74, 93.
Cross, Noah, 42.
Crozer, Mrs. John P., 125, 127.
Crozer, Mr. Samuel A., 127, 138.
Crozer Theological Seminary, 94, 121, 124, 128, 134.

D.

DAGG, JOHN L., D. D., 69, 70.
Dale, Mr., 87, 88.
Darby, Susan, 97.
Davis, Mr., 15.
Davis, Rev. David, 20, 32, 33, 54, 55.
Davis, Rev. Hugh, 32.
Davis, Rev. John, 54.
Davis, Rev. Noah, 23.
Davis, Rev. William, 33.
Dazey, Rev. Eliphaz, 27, 31, 33, 36, 43, 45.
Decline of Baptist Churches in Delaware, causes of, 78.
Deitz, Rev. Charles M., 139.
Delaware Association, 38, 48, 50, 51, 61, 72, 74–96.
Delaware Association, new, proposed, 132.
Delaware Avenue Church, Wilmington, 112, 115, 127, 130, 139.
Delaware Baptist Missionary Union, 132, 140.
——, ladies' meeting in behalf of, 138.
Delaware Bible Society, 84.
Delaware, first Baptist churches in, 10.
Delaware, freedom of Baptists in, 25.
Delaware, lesson of Baptist History in, 7.
Delaware, needs of, 8.
Delaware Society for Domestic Missions, 84, 87.
Dennison, Rev. C. W., 101.
Der Sendbote, 111.
Dewees, Col., 57.
Dewees, Cornelius, 34, 35.
Dewees, Rev. Joshua, 31, 36.
Dickerson, J. S., D. D., 101.
Dickinson, E. W., D. D., 132, 142.
Dingle, Rev. Edward Carter, 27, 30.
Disputation between Abel Morgan and Samuel Finley, 53.
Dobbins, Rev. Frank S., 72.
Dodge, Daniel, D. D., 47, 48, 61, 82, 83, 141.
Dover Church, 103–107, 120, 121, 132, 137.
Dowen, Rev. Z. T., 134.
Downer, Rev. J. R., 135, 138.
Dutch Creek Church, 15, 31, 39, 74.
Duffee, Deacon, 137.
Duval, Rev. B. F., 44.
Dwyer, Rev. W. H. H., 117.
Dyer, Rev. S., Ph. D., 138.

E.

EARLE, A. B., D. D., 116.
Earle, Alfred, 50.
Earle, C. C., 140.
Earle, Samuel, 50.
East Landing Church, 32.
Eastwood, Rev. Thomas M., 123, 128, 129, 134, 136, 139, 140.
Eaton, Rev. Isaac, A. M., 55.
Edwards, Rev. Morgan, A. M.,

16, 18, 19, 24, 25, 27, 29, 31, 34, 36, 37, 39, 40, 41, 44, 45, 58–60, 75, 81.
Ellis, John, 46.
Elm Street Church, Wilmington, 123, 128, 129, 130.
Emmons, Harry, 137.
Evans, Mr., 15.
Evans, Rev. Thomas, 53.

F.

FARRELL, Rev. GIDEON, 21, 27, 31, 33, 34, 46, 63, 69.
Farrell, Mary, 63.
Fellman, Rev. J., 112.
Ferris, Mrs., 42.
Fifth Church, Philadelphia, 64.
Finley, Rev. Samuel, 53.
First Church, Philadelphia, 52, 59.
First Church, Wilmington, 40, 50, 76, 77, 84, 92, 102, 113, 123, 127.
First German Church, Philadelphia, 109.
First German Church, Wilmington, 107–112.
First Presbyterian Church, Wilmington, 44.
Fleeson, Rev. Thomas, 23, 30, 32, 34, 36, 41, 42, 43, 44, 45.
Fleischman, Rev. Conrad, 109, 110.
Fletcher, Rev. Leonard, 97.
Flippo, Rev. O. F., 105, 106, 118, 119, 120, 121, 122, 130, 132.
Flood, Rev. Joseph, 30, 36, 46.
Folwell, Rev. George W., 51, 114, 118, 121, 132, 138.
Fouling Creek, Maryland, 26, 28.
Frame, Miles P., 137.

Franklin, Benjamin, 54.
Freehold Church, New Jersey, 55.
Friendship Engine-house, meeting in, 12.
Fulton, J. D., D. D., 8.

G.

GALBRAITH, JOHN, 127.
Gano, Rev. John, 55.
Garrett, Mr. W. E., 127.
Gartside, Mr. Benjamin, Sr., 127, 137.
Gates, General, 58.
Gawthrop, Alfred, Esq., 100, 118, 138.
George, J. H., 137.
George, Mrs. Jonathan, 125.
Georgetown Church, 32.
German Baptist Church, Brooklyn, N. Y., 107.
German Baptists, connection of, with Delaware Baptists, 71.
German Church, Wilmington, 71.
Gibbins, Rev. John, 27, 28.
Gibbins, Rev. Jonathan, 27, 30, 37.
Gibbins, Deacon Joshua, 30.
Gibbins, Rev. Samuel, 27, 29.
Gilbert, Rev. Curtis, 43.
Gill, Dr. John, of London, 59.
Gill, Rev. T. A., U. S. N., 114.
Gillette, A. D., D. D., 80, 104.
Gospel Church, a, 42.
Grafton, Elder William, 22.
Graham, Sarah A., 97.
Gravelly Branch Church, 28, 30, 37, 39, 75, 77.
Great Valley Church, Pennsylvania, 32, 55, 56, 61.
Green, Rev. Samuel R., 48, 84.
Greene, Rev. David, 85.

INDEX. 151

Gregg, Lucy V., 112, 127.
Gregg, William H., 112, 113, 127, 130, 137.
Griffith, Rev. Benjamin, of Montgomery Church, 20.
Griffith, Benjamin, D. D., 99.
Griffith, Rev. Thomas, 14, 19.
Griffiths, Abel, 43.
Grimmell, Jeremiah, 71, 107, 108, 110.
Grimmell, Rev. Julius C., 107.
Grimmell, Margaret, 110.

H.
HALDEMAN, Rev. ISAAC M., 114, 139.
Harker, Rev. Samuel, 54, 87.
Harper, Rev. H. B., 135, 139, 140.
Harris, Samuel, 24.
Harrison, Rev. Charles, 107.
Haselhuhn, Rev. J. C., 111.
Haswell, Rev. J. M., 116.
Heath, Rev. M., 120, 121, 122, 131, 138.
Heazlet, John, 97.
Hera, Rev. E. R., 104.
Heyburn, G. E., 137.
Hirzel, Mrs. Theresa, 111.
Historical Society of Delaware, 44.
History, what it is, 6.
Hodgman, Mr. S. A., 100.
Hoefflin, Rev. J. M., 107, 108, 112, 139.
Hopkins, Rev. C. J., 105.
Hopkins, Elizabeth, 43.
Hope, Rev. J. M., 118, 119, 120, 121, 122, 139.
Housel, Wilson, 50.
Howe, General, 58.
Hudson River Association, 90, 92.
Hughes, Evan David, 33.
Hughes, Rev. Philip, 21, 22, 25, 26, 27, 28, 30, 34, 37, 39, 40, 42, 43, 44, 96, 106.
Hyatt, James, 33.

I.
IMPOSITION of hands, introduction of, 17.
Independents, the, 32.
Iron Hill Meeting-house, 15.
Irving, James, 137.

J.
JAMES, E. F., 138.
James, James, 16.
James, Maury, 130.
James, Rev. Owen, 138.
James, Philip, 16.
Jerseys, the, 18.
Johnson, G. J., D. D., 138.
Johnson, Rev. Jethro, 72, 86, 87.
Jones, Rev. David, A. M., 45, 55–58.
Jones, Eleanor Evans, 55.
Jones, Rev. Griffith, 33.
Jones, Horatio Gates, D. D., 55.
Jones, Hon. H. G., 55, 58.
Jones, Rev. James, 33.
Jones, Rev. Jenkin, 52.
Jones, Rev. Miller, 139.
Jones, Morgan, 55.
Jones, Rev. P. L., 134.
Jones, Samuel, D. D., 45, 53.
Jones, Mr. Washington, 98, 99, 100, 130, 137, 138.
Jones, Mr. William G., 99, 102, 141.

K.
KAISER, Mrs. ELIZABETH, 111.
Kalley, Walter, 140.
Kees, Thomas C., 112.

152 INDEX.

Kelsay, Rev. R., 30.
Kennard, Joseph H., D. D., 50, 61, 97.
Kennard, J. Spencer, D. D., 63.
King, Peter, 35.
Kitts, Rev. Thomas J., 48, 61, 141.
Knapp, Elder Jacob, 100, 101.
Knowlton, Mrs. M. J., 138.

L.

LEACH, Rev. SANDFORD, 100, 101.
Leamy, Rev. Henry H., 146.
Lehmann's "Baptist Churches in Germany," 66.
LeMaistre, George A., 100.
LeMaistre, Mrs. George A., 138.
Lemon, Dr. Robert, 24, 96.
Lewis, Rev. Daniel, 141.
Lewis, Rev. David, 49.
Lewisburg University, 128.
Lincoln Church, 117, 118, 122.
Little Creek Church, 76, 77.
London Tract Church, Pennsylvania, 15, 44.
Long, Prof. J. C., D. D., 138.
Lord's Supper administered in private houses, 33.
Louden, Mr., 38.
Lower Dublin Church, 10, 52.
Lower Saxony Tract Society, 68.
Lunsford, Rev. Lewis, 26.

M.

MACK, Deacon F. C., 116, 137.
Maclay, Dr., 68.
MacMackin, Rev. B., 124, 126, 134, 139.
Madison University, 131.

Maginn, Eugene, 140.
Magnolia Church, 117, 121, 122, 139.
Magonagill, Beulah, 104.
Manning, Dr. James, 53.
Marcus Hook Church, 102, 139, 141.
Marsh, Rev. W. H. H., 51, 101, 118, 132.
Maryatt, Rev. E. E., 121, 128.
Matthews, William, 50.
Mattson, Mary, 43.
McArthur, Rev. Alexander, 101, 135, 138.
McCollin, Mrs. P. G., 138.
McDowel, Mr. Philip, 114.
McKannan, Rev. Mr., 42, 43, 44.
McKeever, F. G., 140.
McKim, John, 43.
McLaughlin, Rev. James, 42, 43.
Media Baptist Church, Pennsylvania, 136, 139.
Meredith, Job, Sr., 31.
Meredith, Luff, 31.
Meredith, Rev. Peter, 36, 93.
Merriken, Rev. Richard H., 119.
Middletown Church, New Jersey, 53.
Miles, Rev. George I., 97.
Miles, Richard, 18.
Milford Church, 118, 122, 136, 139, 146.
Miller, Rev. John, 50.
Miller, Mrs. S. M., 138.
Millsborough Church, 77.
Mispillion Church, 15, 34, 36, 39, 74, 75, 77.
Missionary Societies in Delaware, decline of, 90–96.
Missionary Society in Delaware, 82–90.

INDEX. 153

Missionary spirit, necessity of, 144.
Montgomery Church, Pa., 20.
Moore, Rev. B. T., 124, 139.
Moore, Marion, 112.
Morgan, Rev. Abel, translates the Confession, 17.
Morgan, Rev. Abel, Jr., A. M., 16, 53, 54, 55, 60.
Morgan ap Rhyddarch, 20.
Morgan, Rev. Enoch, 20, 32.
Morton, David, 38.
Mount Moriah, see Cow Marsh.
Mount Zion Church, Independent, 32.
Mühlhausen, John, 111.
Mühlhausen, Sophia, 111.

N.

NAYLOR, Rev. N. C., 106, 123.
Neutze, Frederick, 111.
Newark Academy, 34.
New Castle Church, 124–127, 139.
New Jersey Association, 90, 92.
New Market Street (Fourth) Church, Philadelphia, 62.
New York Association, 90, 92.
Nichols, Rev. D. A., 104, 105.

O.

OLD SCHOOL BAPTISTS, 140.
Old School and New School Baptists, 94, 95.
Old Swedes' Church, Wilmington, 10.
Oncken, John G., D. D., 65–71, 108.
Owens, Dr. Frederick, 137.

P.

PAOLI, massacre at, 58.
Parham, Miss E. C., 117.

Parker, Rev. B. G., 107, 134, 135, 136, 139.
Parris, George, 103, 104, 136, 137, 140.
Parris, Jane E., 104.
Parsons, Mr., 32.
Patten, Rev. John, 33, 34.
Peck, John M., D. D., 72.
Peckworth, Rev. John P., 49, 50, 82.
Pencader Academy, 53.
Pendleton, J. M., D. D., 138.
Penn, Admiral, 25.
Penn, William, advocates liberty of conscience, 25.
———, landing of, 10.
———, purchase of land from, 15.
Pennsylvania General Association, 62.
Pennypack Church, 14, 18.
Pepper, Prof. G. D. B., D. D., 135, 138.
Pepper, Mrs. G. D. B., 138.
Phœnix Engine-house, meetings in, 113.
Philadelphia Association, 17, 20, 31, 33, 34, 43, 48, 50, 51, 52, 61, 74, 75, 80, 90, 92, 97, 101, 113, 115, 123, 124, 128, 132.
———, Delaware churches connected with, 140.
———, first printing of Minutes by, 60.
Philadelphia, First Church, 40, 49.
Piepgrass, Rev. R., 111.
Piscataway Church, New Jersey, 48.
Plymouth Church, 115–117, 122.
Pollard, Rev. John, 30.
Porter, Mr., 38.

154 INDEX.

Presbyterians, Baptist Church in Wilmington established by, 41.
Princeton College, New Jersey, 54.
Probasco, Mr. R. W. L., 132.
Pulpit, movable, in private houses, 37.
Purinton, Rev. D. B., 105, 115, 116, 117, 118.
Putnam, Rev. H. C., 165.

Q.
QUEEN ANNE'S CHURCH, 74.
Quinby, Edgar H., 100.

R.
RADNOR CHURCH, Pennsylvania, 18.
Ransom, Elder Elisha, 48.
Read, Rev. J. S., 139.
Read, Mr. Miles S., 121.
Read, Mr. William S., 121.
Reader, Rev. J. J., 107.
Redman, John, 42, 43.
Rhees, Morgan J., D. D., 78, 98, 100.
Rhode Island College, see Brown University, 29.
Rice, Mr., 83.
Ridley Church, Pa., 139.
Rittenhouse, Elder E., 50, 77.
Robinson, Rev. William K., 22, 92.
Rogers, William, D. D., 75.
Rowanty Church, 26.
Roxborough Church, Pa., 46.
Russell, William, 137.

S.
SALISBURY, birthplace of Rev. Noah Davis, 23.
Salisbury Association, 23, 27, 34, 37, 75, 76, 77.
Salisbury, Mr. E. H., 117, 137.
Salisbury, Rev. E. P., 116, 117.
Salisbury, Mrs. E. P., 117.
Sansom Street Church, Philadelphia, 64, 65, 70.
Schuylkill, baptism in the, 46.
Schwager, Elizabeth, 111.
Schwager, Mr. John, 109, 111.
Scott, Mr., 93.
Sears, Barnas, D. D., LL.D., 66, 68.
Second Church, Boston, Mass., 54.
Second Church, Hopewell, New Jersey, 62.
Second Church, Philadelphia, 48, 61.
Second Church, Wilmington, 96–102, 103, 109, 110, 112, 113, 134.
Semple, Miss Anne, 65, 108, 110, 112, 113.
Semple, Rev. R. B., 24.
Semple's History, 96.
Separate Baptists, 23.
Shaffer. ——, 122.
Shanafelt, Rev. A. F., 121.
Shiloh Church, Wilmington, 123, 139.
Singing, introduction of, 16, 17.
Slack, Mary, 112, 113.
Smart, Joseph, 50.
Smith, Elnathan, 137.
Smith, J. Wheaton, D. D., 133, 134.
Smith, Mary, 112.
Smith, Robert, 42, 43.
Snead, Rev. S., 36.
Society for the Propagation of the Faith in Foreign Parts, 81.
Sounds, the, Church, 27, 28, 39, 75, 77.

INDEX. 155

South Carolina, church formed in, 15, 16.
South Philadelphia Association, considered, 133.
Southampton Church, Pennsylvania, 55.
Spencer, Rev. David, 46, 55, 138.
Spencer, Rev. W. H., 117, 118, 119.
Springer, Margaret, 97.
Stadiger, Mr. J. J., 127.
Statistics of Delaware Baptist Churches, 143.
Staton, Elder G. W., 22.
Staughton, William, D. D., 83, 141.
Steele, Rev. Isaac, 30.
Steelman, Rev. H., 139.
Sterrett, Margaret, 97.
Stettzer, Mrs., 35.
Stewart, A. B., 137.
Stites, Jonathan, 103, 104.
Stites, Mary, 103, 104.
Stow, Mr. John, 40, 43.
Stow, Sarah, 43.
Stow, Thomas, 43.
Street, George, 140.
Stroud, Mary E., 97.
Strumpfer, Rev. John D., 49.
Sullivan, Rev. J. Wesley, 139.
Sutton, Rev. John, 21, 30, 33.
Swaim, Thomas, D. D., 122, 138.

T.
Tage, J. M., 137.
Taylor, J. B. D. D., 23.
——, his History of Virginia Baptists, 96.
Tenth Church, Philadelphia, 62.
Third Church, Philadelphia, 49.

Thomas, Rev. A. G., 135, 136, 139.
Thomas, Rev. B. D., 64.
Thomas, Rev. Elisha, 19.
Thomas, Rev. Owen, 20.
Thompson, Rev. David, 26.
Thompson, Rev. John P., 103.
Thorne, Rev. Levi, 146.
Tindall, Gideon F., 97.
Todd, Sally Ann, 97.
Tomlinson, Joseph, 43.
Townsend, Charles, 112.
Trevor, M. K., M. D., 142.
Trott, Rev. Samuel, 22, 90.
Trumpp, Rev. H., 111.
Tubbs, Captain Calvin, 63–71, 72.
Tubbs, Calvin, Jr., 67.
Tubbs, Samuel Welsh, 67.
Tull, Mr., 27.
Turley, Captain E., 65.

U.
University of Pennsylvania, 54.
Ustick, Rev. Thomas, 49, 95.

V.
Village Green Church, 139.
Vreeland, Rev. P. S., 138.

W.
Walker, Elizabeth, 104.
Walker, Rev. Henry, 42, 43.
Walker, Rev. Joseph, 140–143.
Walter, Rev. John P., 103, 104.
Warren, Jonah G., D. D., 70.
Waters, Rev. James, 101, 121.
Watts, Brother, 18.
Way, Mrs. Elizabeth, 40, 43.
Wayland, H. L., D. D., 138.
Wayland Seminary, Washington, D. C., 124.

INDEX.

Wayne, General Anthony, 58.
Webb, A. M., 117, 118, 122.
Welsh Concordance, 20.
Welsh, Hon. John, 67.
Welsh, John, Esq., 65.
Welsh Neck Association, 16.
Welsh Neck Church, South Carolina, 16.
Welsh Tract, 15.
Welsh Tract Church, 14, 15, 18, 19, 30, 40, 42, 52, 53, 54, 55, 63, 74, 76, 77, 80, 83, 84, 90, 92.
——, branches of, 31.
——, out-stations of, 38.
Welsh Tract Church Book, 17.
Weston, President H.G., D.D., 134, 138.
Weston, Dr. J. B., 137.
Wilegoos, Mr., 27.
Williams, C. F., 140.
Williams, Thomas, 43.
Williamsburg Church, 108.
Willis, Mr., 15.
Willis, Rev. ——, 26.
Willis, John, 37.
Wilmington, origin of Baptists in, 39.
Wilmington, First Church, 15, 48, 50, 61, 74, 97.
Wilmington, First German Church, 139.
Wilmington, Second Church formed, 92.
Wilmington Institute, 113.
Winter, Thomas, D. D., 51.
Women collectors for Domestic Missions, 84.
Woolford, Rev. Stephen W., 21, 87, 88.
Woolsey, Rev. James J., 97.
Worth, Rev. William, 30.
Wright, Rev. T. G., 136, 139.
Wyoming Church, 120, 121, 139.
Wyoming Institute, 105, 106, 121, 130.

Y.

YORKTOWN, 58.
Young, Rev. William H., 124, 126, 136, 137.

Z.

ZION CHURCH, 118–120, 121, 123, 139.

THE END.